BE

A. C. PING has traveled extensively and
lived and worked in the United Kingdom,
Africa, and Australia.

He has been many things, including
a futures trader, a limo driver, a teacher,
a scuba divemaster, a tour guide, and
a corporate consultant.

Now he writes about new ways
of living and working and assists
individuals and organizations in making
their bold visions become reality.

BE

A. C. Ping

MARLOWE & COMPANY
NEW YORK

AVALON
publishing group incorporated

First published by Ricochet Productions in Australia in 2001.
Previously published by Penguin Books Australia Ltd. in
Australia in 2003.

Library of Congress Control Number: 2004109245

ISBN 1-56924-422-7

9 8 7 6 5 4 3 2 1

Cover designed by John Papailiou

Interior designed by Pauline Neuwirth, Neuwirth & Associates, Inc.

Printed in Canada

for dorle

■

acknowledgments

Lots of people's energies flow into
and intermingle in this book!

Thanks to all the people who were willing to
ask the thoughtful questions: Matt, Sofi,
Dorle, Lindy, Miriam, Keith, and Anna.
I can look back and see your wisdom
and good intentions.

To those who were willing to be the guinea pigs:
Shannon, Katherine, Stevie, Jono, Lotus, Lucinda,
and Carlos. You opened my eyes to
different perspectives and I am grateful for
your time and input.

Finally, it takes not only belief but a
conscious decision to act to bring a book
like this to completion. So I am indebted to
Barbara, Ruth, and Priscilla. Your passion
and support inspires me to greater things.

A. C. Ping

contents

BE

introduction

What we do in life,
echoes in eternity.
—Maximus, *Gladiator*

at the start of the movie *Gladiator*, Russell Crowe's character Maximus is a celebrated Roman general who commands the respect of both his troops and his Caesar. As an instrument of power in a hierarchical structure, his role is clear. But within just a few scenes he is forced to take a stand for what he believes in, and his world is turned upside down.

Betrayed by a man he saw as his brother, sentenced to an unjust death, and late witness to the brutal slaying of his family, he has a new purpose . . . *vengeance*. Vengeance not driven by spite or jealousy, but by the desire for justice.

As he sets out to fulfill his new purpose, Maximus shows that he is guided by clear principles. He refuses to kill a man in cold blood just to please the crowd, he rallies his fellow slaves together for their mutual benefit, and he remains true to those who have helped him.

Finally, he sacrifices himself for the good of the Roman people, dying in battle, the victor over tyranny and injustice.

If only life were so clear-cut.

Gladiator shows us in two hours how simple life can be if we can answer three key questions: *What is my purpose? What do I believe in?* and *How can I transcend the self?*

In these times of ever-expanding choice, few of us can answer those three questions with absolute clarity. Sure, there are still places like the jungles of Africa and South America where life can be broken down into a simple equation. But how many people would trade first-world luxury for third-world clarity? The paradox of our times is that we have created societies that satisfy basic needs and to a large extent eliminate life and death issues, yet depression spreads like a festering sore and individuals seek solace in drugs and suicide.

As we strive to know more, to have more, and to do more, in many cases we have become less. In defining our worth through the value of our possessions and the strength of our achievements we have neglected to address the question of who we are being. Even as we find

a moment to ponder the question of who we are, we quickly fill the void with the propaganda that is perpetrated upon us by the media and the arms of the state, which seek to inculcate us as mere cogs in the economic machine.

But there is change afoot! We stand at the brink of a new age, and more people are choosing to question the mindlessness of our times. Instead of taking things for granted and following the pack along a well-worn but unfulfilling path, some have chosen to say "Stop!"

This book is for those people—maybe that's you? If it is, I hope this book helps you. Its aim is to help you to address those three questions mentioned above, that is, *What is my purpose? What do I believe in?* and *How do I transcend the self?* In addition, this book considers the question *How can I be happy?* Because a clear purpose in life will provide direction, but it won't necessarily provide happiness.

how did this book come into being?

Well, let's just say that ten years ago my life was traveling along quite nicely. I was married and looking for a nice house to buy, my career as a finance wizard was on the fast track, my friends and family were supportive, and my only concern was whether I should trade the BMW for a Porsche.

Then the shit hit the fan. . . . In the space of three years, I had what my friends love to tell me was my early midlife crisis and quit my job. My father-in-law, who I was very close to, died suddenly and painfully from a terminal illness. My marriage fell apart. The BMW was sold. A close friend I'd grown up with died of a heart attack just before his thirtieth birthday. And in the midst of all that, my friends and family questioned what the hell I was doing with my life and effectively threw the self-doubt gremlin into my mind.

To say that I was taken aback would be a major understatement. My beautifully planned life was in tatters and all anybody seemed to be doing was pointing the finger at me and saying, *What have you done*?

So, I learned right there that the best lesson you can learn in life is how to pick yourself up off the floor, dust yourself off, and get on with things, because if there's one certainty in life, it's that you'll get knocked down many times.

In the seven years since, it's a skill I've had lots of practice at. But every time I've been knocked down I've tried to learn something from it and now I'd like to share. . . .

The book is divided into three parts: **BE YOU**, **BE HAPPY,** and **BE ONE**. It's not the be-all and end-all. It's not a textbook or an instruction book for life. It won't

give you the answers but it will prompt you to ask some questions that may lead you to your answers. If it makes you think, then it's achieved the purpose I set for it. That's all I ask.

BE *you*

driven to distraction

ever wondered about the meaning of life? About what we're doing here? The point of it all? I have. It's something that's bugged me from an early age. I like to have meaning, I like to have clear tasks, I hate it when no one knows what's going on. I used to ask my parents what I was doing here and it pissed me off when they said, "You can do anything you want to do, as long as you set your mind to it."

Okay, yeah, neat answer, but it doesn't give me any more clarity than I had before. Are you guys just messing with my head or do you really not know? Those kids at school who knew what they wanted to be annoyed me too! How can you know you want to be a doctor when you're twelve years old? Did your parents tell you that? Did you ever think to question them? Tell me the truth, I want to know!

But seriously, *Who am I?* and *What is my life's purpose?* are outrageously BIG questions. Mostly, we never get a good chance to answer them. Society tells us that we must first complete ten to twelve years of schooling—Task 1. Then we must find a useful role to play in the economic system so we can support ourselves—Task 2. If we complete Task 1 well, then we get more study, to do and, theoretically at least, Task 2 becomes easier. If we complete Task 2 well, then we have more than enough to support ourselves and we get to Task 3—have a family.

If we just stick to Tasks 1, 2, and 3 we can effectively avoid ever asking the questions *Who am I?* and *What is my life's purpose?* by losing ourselves in the distractions of daily existence. At school we can study hard, play sports, and experiment with sex. In the workforce we can work sixty-hour weeks to climb the corporate ladder, join the social club, and plot our next career move. Once the partner and kids come along, the possibilities for distraction are endless—dinner parties, family outings, parents' nights, and so on.

But at some point along this continuum, most people suffer a crisis of meaning. That's the point where they stop and ask—*What's the point?* Generally something triggers it—being dumped by the first girlfriend or boyfriend, being retrenched at work, finding out you can't have kids, or experiencing the death of someone close to you.

I've already mentioned that for me it was an accumulation of things but there is one event that sticks in my mind—the Gulf War in 1991. Picture this—there we were sitting in our plush fifty-third-floor financial headquarters, with a view down the coast through floor-to-ceiling glass on one side, and a big screen TV broadcasting live war footage on the other. And suddenly we'd become military experts, speculating on whether the United States was about to get itself into another Vietnam or if it would be short and sweet. Did we care about the people being killed? Don't be ridiculous! All we wanted to know was whether or not Iraq would hinder the flow of oil from the Middle East, hence damaging Japan's oil-dependent economy. It was like watching a boxing match on TV in a front bar. You know, "I'll take the guy in the blue shorts for a hundred bucks."

A lot of money was made and lost on that war. It was the type of event in which we, as futures traders, took great delight because of the chaos it caused and the opportunities it presented. But for me it was about then that the deep-seated futility of it started to tear apart my psyche. How could I delight in war? What had happened to bring me to that point? I had to stop and reassess what I was doing.

Because of the changing nature of the world, these crises seem to be getting more frequent.

Thirty years ago, if you were male, you could go through school, have a range of jobs to choose from when you finished, pick one to keep for life, choose a bride you could support on a forty-hour-week wage, have three kids, and live happily ever after.

If you were female, you could go through school, learn the secret family cooking recipes, be wooed by a man, raise some kids, and play a key role in the local community.

The big issues were: where to buy a house—generally halfway between the two parents' houses; where to send the kids to school—where you went; and where to go for school holidays. Oh and don't even imagine supporting any sports teams other than the ones your dad supports.

These days, completing school is no guarantee of a job, the average person will have at least seven careers, the forty-hour week is a myth, single-income families are a rarity, and more and more couples are choosing not to have kids. Not to mention information overload, the greenhouse effect, and globalization. Phew. . . . It's exhausting just thinking about it!

So, how to deal with it? Escape, that's the key, or at least it seems to be. Take the edge off. Have a few drinks at the end of a twelve-hour day, smoke a joint on the way home from work, pop an E at the weekend, snort a line or two before going out to dinner . . . Wake up in the morning and do it all again. . . . Feel bad? Take something to feel good. . . . Feel good? Take something to feel better. . . .

Anything but look the demon of emptiness in the eye. Keep the stopper pushed down hard. Trap the genie in the bottle. Tomorrow brings a whole new day, gotta be better than today. Maybe it will all disappear. Life's meant to be good isn't it? If it's all a lie I may as well die. . . .

take a pill? no way!

SO, let's suppose there is some reason for it all, because if there's not then you may as well indulge in hedonism. Have all the pleasure you can get, take all the drugs you can take, experience all the thrills you can stomach. Guess what? At the end of the day you're still left with what's right in front of you, ready or not.

If you're reading this book, you've probably come to accept that there's no way to escape on a permanent basis. Hell, even suicide lands you right back here if you believe in reincarnation.

So, is there a point? Gotta be, or read no further.

From a Christian perspective, we're here to do God's will and if we're good we get to ascend to the Kingdom of Heaven. From a Buddhist perspective, we're here to become enlightened and be released from this world of suffering. From a spiritual perspective, we're here to learn the lessons we need to learn so that we can grow spiritually and escape this physical realm.

All sounds pretty similar doesn't it?

The bottom line is this. Make a decision. Either there is no purpose to life, in which case you should be driven by your base desires and accept short-term pleasure along with ongoing pain. Or, decide that there is some purpose to life, in which case you should break the spiral of short-term escapism, accept the current sense of emptiness and start doing some work to fill in the hole. If your reality is no good then make your reality better. Don't just escape, because when you come back—and you always do—you'll be faced with the same thing, over and over again.

Interestingly, if you ask a room full of people if they believe they have a specific purpose in this life, about seventy percent will say yes. The distressing part is that a much smaller percentage are able to tell you what it is. . . .

Okay, okay, so how do you do it? How do you work out what your purpose is?

Well, first, let's digress a little and look at the nature of existence. We need a few clues to the sort of questions we could ask to find our life's purpose. If we decide that there is a life's purpose, we almost have to assume that there is a "higher force" or creator. I know this is a bit tautological, but look at it this way. If there is a purpose to life then who decided it? If you decided on your own life's purpose before you came into this world, then that presupposes three things: 1—reincarnation, 2—you have a "higher self" that already knows what your life's purpose is, and 3—that there is another realm of existence. So, then the question is: *How can you "talk" to this "higher" part of yourself?*

If somebody or something decided on your life's purpose for you then surely they would want you to find out what it is? Otherwise what's the point? Again, how do we "talk" to this "higher being"?

Assuming, for the moment, that we can't just pick up the phone to chat with this "higher being" and find out what our purpose is in life, what sort of things might point us in the right direction? Surely there must be some clues?

Logic isn't really going to help us. Using logic, we could choose any sort of life's purpose and then rationalize it. For example, could our life's purpose be to suffer? That'd be a pretty shitty life purpose to choose for yourself, unless there was a benefit to the suffering—then it would be logical. The problem with logic is that the "lower" self controls it. That is, we have control over our rational/logical function the entire time—there are no surprises. Any answers can only come from us and we don't know. . . .

To tap into a "higher" self we need to tap into something that has no sense of logic to it. That is, it must just seem right or feel right. This is where we can use our emotions to guide us, and where passion is all-powerful.

The world we have created is based firmly on logic and rational thinking, as espoused by Aristotle, Socrates, and Plato so many years ago. To the rational mind, something either is or isn't and there is nothing in between. Our world reflects this through the systems we have set up. Logically, you should go to school, get good grades, go to college, get a good degree, go into the workplace, then work hard and be happy.

The only problem is that happiness isn't logical.

How many people do you know who have left high-paying careers to pursue a life's passion for painting, writing, or singing? How many are happier now?

My point is that the rational world is full of holes. Logic assumes that we can create happiness by mixing together some ingredients. This is the same logic that mixes together chemical ingredients to make pills like ecstasy—happiness, yes, but only for a while.

So, back to that question about life's purpose. I suppose you've guessed by now that there isn't a step-by-step logical process to follow. But there are clues along the way—most significantly, *Passion points to purpose.*

be still

if we are able to talk to our higher selves when we arrive in this world, one thing is for sure—we get it beaten out of us as soon as possible. "Conform, conform, conform, be one of us, don't be different," society screams at us. We are told how to walk, how to talk, what's right, what's wrong, who's good, who's bad, what we should aspire to, and what we should desire. Buy into the system as soon as possible.

A world based on desire might give us short-term goals but it is bereft of meaning. We believe we are free but we're slaves to consumerism. The very means of survival have been taken away from the individual and placed firmly within the economic system. If we are focused on just surviving we have no time to contemplate meaning.

BE

The first step toward liberation is to tear away the layers of brainwashing that create this fixed view of the world so that we can find our true selves. Should, shouldn't, can, can't, do, don't, right, wrong, is, isn't, STOP!

Most of us are so brainwashed that before we can even get a thought out we're reacting. Living a life of meaning is about freedom—the freedom to choose how to act in any situation. Not just reacting mindlessly to everything you come in contact with. We're told from an early age that the world is a certain way. Then we try to live our lives according to that definition—always assuming that someone out there actually knows what it's all about.

CRAP!

The world is a mystery. We should never stop asking but we should never expect to know the answer. Anyone who tells you otherwise is full of it!

So, back to this meaning thing.

First, get your mind to the stage where you stop reacting mindlessly to things. Be still.

Imagine that your mind is a glass of silty water being carried by a monkey swinging from branch to branch. (Bizarre image, eh?) Just as the silt begins to settle, the monkey sees something in the next tree and swings over to it, stirring up the silt again in the process. Can you relate to that?

Look at it this way—you decide that you're not happy with the job you've been doing, so you sit down to think about how you could change your life for the better. You're deep in thought when the phone rings. It's one of your best friends and they have a great story to tell you about a guy you've liked for a while. Before you know it you're in the car on the way over to her place to plot your next move.

We have to get the monkey to sit still for a while so the silt can settle in the glass, and the water will become clear. Single point focus is what is needed here—a meditative approach.

When I first learned to meditate I told my mom, who freaked out, thinking I'd joined some weird hippie cult. Even now when I mention meditation, many people have quite a strange reaction. Maybe they see it as a pagan ritual or something. In any case, generally it's a reaction that arises out of fear.

Although there are lots of really weird meditation practices you can do, meditation itself is nothing out of the ordinary. In the dictionary it is defined as "contemplation on a subject." Christian monks have been doing it for years, as have Buddhists, Muslims, and elite athletes. Elite athletes? Yes. Nadia Comaneci, the Romanian gymnast, shocked the world by getting a series of ten out of ten scores at the 1980 Olympics. When asked how she managed to achieve so many perfect results, Nadia answered, "My mind is always full of getting it right." Sounds very meditative to me.

So, meditation—focusing on one thing so that monkey will stop jumping around. I've found the best way to meditate is to find somewhere quiet where there are no distractions and you're unlikely to be disturbed. Inside is generally better than outside because the energy tends to be calmer.

Sit quietly with your back straight and your legs crossed. This is not just to be torturous. If you sit with your back straight you align all of the energy centers, or chakras, in the body. From a Yin and Yang perspective, we are the bridge between Heaven and Earth—the Chi, or life force, flows in through the top of our head, down through our body and out into the earth.

Once you are comfortable, focus your mind on one thing. This can be a mantra, which you repeat over and over again; an image, which you concentrate on; or a thing, like your breath. Personally, I like the breath—because breathing is an unconscious action. By focusing on the breath, you link mind and body. To help you focus on the breath, concentrate on the touch of the breath on your top lip as you breathe in and out. Initially you may have to either breathe hard or wet your top lip to feel the touch of the breath, but eventually your mind will become sharper and it will become easier.

Now, remember that what we are trying to do is stabilize the mind so that we can tap into our true nature. Visualize that silt sinking slowly to the bottom of the glass and focus your mind gently on the touch of the breath. And you will find that after a very short space of time, your mind has wandered off. You may not even realize that it has happened until you're several thoughts away.

For example, you start meditating and a thought pops into your head about what you're going to have for dinner. Then you realize that you haven't had dinner with your parents for a while. Then you remember the last time you had dinner with them and recall how good the dessert was. Then you remember that you meant to ask your mother for the recipe. Suddenly you remember that you're supposed to be meditating and you get annoyed with yourself for being so useless that you can't even focus on one thing for five minutes. A voice inside your head says, "This is too hard, meditation is for those hippie people who are probably stoned when they do it anyway so they're cheating. Why not just forget about all this and go and have a drink with some friends at the bar?"

Gentleness is the trick! For a long time your mind has been allowed to do whatever it wanted, the monkey has been exploring wherever it pleased. It's been swinging you around, not the reverse. You can't change all that overnight and getting angry with yourself will only make it harder.

Humor and gentleness are much kinder masters. Anyone can meditate, it just takes a bit of time to settle into it. When you find that your mind has wandered off, just chuckle to yourself and gently come back to the breath. After a while you will find that you can focus on the breath for longer and longer periods without wandering off. What you will also find is that more and more of that silt will sink to the bottom and your mind will become clearer and clearer.

This is the first step, and maybe one of the hardest, toward finding meaning. Finding a degree of space and clarity.

Meditation doesn't have to happen sitting down. It can be done while walking, running, riding, and in the midst of many other pursuits. Remember, all you're trying to do by meditating is calm and focus the mind. You can do this as you go for your daily walk. Instead of allowing your mind to wander aimlessly, focus your eyes on a point in front of your feet (be careful not to run into any poles!) and visualize that silt sinking to the bottom of the glass. Or run, concentrating just on your breathing (and ditto for the pole thing!).

The more you meditate, the more you'll find a calm space within yourself. Here you can contemplate your life free from the chatter of society. Now you're in a good space for finding passion.

finding passion

Whatever you decide to do in life,
just be passionate about it . . .
Don't be intimidated by competition,
as success is sweeter and failure less bitter
when you have given everything. You have to
be true to yourself—it's your life. You are the
masters of your destiny, and passion,
not pedigree, will win in the end.
—JON BON JOVI, Oxford Union debating society, 2001

no, I'm not talking about a sex thing, although that is good too! I'm talking about finding out what things in your life trigger a strong emotion. Passion is a good indication of purpose because it's so irrational. I know people who get passionate about stamps, trees, bugs, bees, boats, bears. . . . The list could go on forever.

As you've probably gathered, I'm passionate about the meaning of existence.

Passion is great because it breaks down the linear understanding of existence into which our society tries so hard to indoctrinate people. We are told from an early age that we must do this, or do that. We are given tasks that we must accomplish and we are measured or judged by how well we do. Which box do you fit into? Good, bad, or mediocre?

> Where the spirit does not work with
> the hand, there is no art.
> —LEONARDO DA VINCI

In this sense, life becomes very linear or one-directional. It's hard just to be when someone is always asking you what you're doing. Passion breaks this down because when you're passionate about something you're happy just to be in it. Of course it's nice to win at something you're passionate about, or be acknowledged for it, but it's not the end of the world if it doesn't happen. If you're living in line with your passion, that's enough.

Let's consider my personal example. I love thinking about all this stuff and writing it all down; something deep within me drives it. I'm always trying to make sense of the world so I'm happy to indulge in this with no particular end in sight. The act is enough for me to get lost in. It can

drive some people a bit crazy, though. My mother got so sick of me asking "Why?" as a little kid that she went out and bought me *The Book of Why*.

Or take sculpture. I know people who sculpt and never sell any of their work, but they love to do it. Or the researcher who spends years and years trying to find the cure for cancer with no success. Passion drives them. They may seem crazy to us but they are as happy as they could possibly be.

When you've found a bit of inner peace through being still, it's time to ask the passion question. The answer may be a surprise but I guarantee you'll get a charge just by acknowledging what you're really passionate about. You may not find an answer right away and you may be distracted by things that you find fun. For instance, I find fun in listening to music but I'm not passionate about it. If I had to listen to music all day every day I'd go crazy. I love to scuba dive, it's a great escapist pursuit that I could become seriously addicted to, but I'm not passionate about it in a life-mission sense.

Write a list of all the things you're passionate about, then start delving into them more deeply. Try and work out which ones are fun, which ones are escapism, and which ones are passion. Oh, and a word of warning, remember that you're stepping out of the box here, away from the fixed view of the world that you're supposed to have. Nobody ever says that life should be driven by passion.

They say things like, "Life is all about hard work," or "Life is about achievement." Don't be surprised if people tell you you're crazy when you mention to them that you want to become an entomologist. . . .

Remember again—be gentle with yourself, this may take time.

I'm passionate about . . .

_____

_____

_____

_____

_____

_____

_____

_____

_____

_____

_____

_____

_____

_____

_____

NOTES

failure is not an option

Our doubts are traitors and make
us lose the good we oft might gain
by fearing to attempt.
—*Measure for Measure*, Shakespeare

what if you try it and it doesn't work? Fear of failure drives many of us. But what would you do if you knew you could not fail? It's another question to ask to help you find purpose.

For the "life force," or maybe we should call it "divine inspiration," to flow through you it must be unimpeded by fear. Fear blocks us up—you know what I mean, the feeling you get when you're about to do something really challenging and all of a sudden it's hard to breathe?

What would you do if you knew you could not fail? This is a good question to ask when faced with challenging decisions. Take fear out of the equation and you're much more likely to get an answer that is closer to your true purpose.

If I knew I couldn't fail I would . . .

_____

_____

_____

_____

_____

_____

_____

_____

_____

_____

_____

_____

_____

NOTES

blinded by mammon?

we live in a world dominated by material desires that can generally only be satisfied by having money, so we can become blinded by Mammon. The pursuit of money can lead you on a merry chase and there are many, many people and institutions in this world that are solely aimed at tying you up along the way.

Although our society is supposedly founded on the ideals of freedom and equality, we've set up a system that aims to take our freedom away from us at every turn. I've already mentioned that the means to a self-sufficient existence have been taken away from us by the state. That is, you can't just decide that you're going to opt out of society and fend for yourself. Head for the hills with your bow and arrow and there'll soon be a search party out to find you and drag you back into this world.

"Who are you?" they'll say. "We'll take you back home and if you have no home to go to we'll look after you."

Instead of being a noble hunter fending for yourself in the wild, you'll become a pitiful beggar lining up for hand-outs at the local charity.

But I digress, let's go back to the money thing. As soon as you get into the workforce, all manner of people and institutions come to you offering to lend you money to purchase tempting goods. Goods that they tell you will show the world that you are a worthy and respected member of society. New cars, stereos, clothes, bikes, and any-thing else you can slap onto your new credit card.

Their aim is to lend you exactly as much as you can afford to repay without running away. They work in cahoots with the people making and advertising the goods. Buy this car and you're a legend; buy these clothes and you're cool, you must be, Elle Macpherson wears them!

Before you know it, your hands are tied. Without even thinking about what you really want to do you've left school, got a job as a bank clerk and now have so much debt that you can't even think about leaving. Next comes resigning yourself to it. Don't worry, there are plenty of people you can whine to about the injustice of life—over a few drinks of course! I know, you'd love to do something you're really passionate about, but you've just got to pay off those damn credit cards first.

Forget it, it doesn't work. Never wait for things to happen, just do. Find out what you're passionate about now, then start working toward it. Don't wait to be free of debt or other commitments before you start. While you have no purpose you're still reactive so what happens is this. You go to work trying to be positive but shit happens and you feel bad at the end of the day. While walking home you see some nice clothes in a shop and the temptation is too great to resist. Once you get home you love the dress but you feel bad that you spent so much money so you go and see some friends, have a few drinks, and whine about the injustice of life. In the morning you battle through your hangover to get up and do it all over again. Sound familiar?

Don't do it anymore! If you're unsure, ask yourself this question: *If you won a million dollars would you still be doing the same thing or would you quit your job?*

If you would quit your job immediately, then what's stopping you? Mammon? Money should serve you, not the other way around.

Have a purpose, so you can work toward getting out of the situation you're in. Don't wait to get out of your current situation before you determine what your purpose is. It won't happen. You need clarity of purpose to sustain you through those bad days and help you resist that new dress, new car, fancy watch, or groovy phone. Above all, don't be sucked into the game. Don't be ruled by money.

embracing death

It is nothing to die.
It's an awful thing never to have lived.
—*Les Miserables*, Victor Hugo

there is an American Indian tribe that believes death follows us around everywhere we go. It is supposed to be just over our left shoulder, and if you look back really quickly you may even get a glimpse of it. Our death follows us, waiting for the right moment. Every now and again, if it sees fit, it taps us on the shoulder to remind us that it is there.

This happened to a friend of mine recently. She'd finished school and was quite content to be working a meaningless job, going out as often as possible with friends to party. Obviously death wasn't too keen on what she was up to—after visiting the doctor for a sore throat and taking some antibiotics, she went into anaphylactic shock. As she drove home her throat started to swell up until she couldn't breathe. She stopped the car and promptly passed out. Luckily someone found her and took her to the doctor where they managed to revive her, but not before she had stopped breathing for a few minutes.

What effect did it have on her? She said she realized how easy it is to die. She thought that there would be some sort of warning before death, you know, being sick for a while, having that scene like in the movies where the doctors, all grave faced, come in and say, "We've got some bad news, you've got six months to live." But, no, just like that, you're dead, no warning, no lights and sirens, nothing, shit. . . .

In the West we like to think we are immortal. We live our lives as if we have plenty of time to do all the things we want to do. Then all of a sudden we're old and near death and we wonder about what might have been, about how things could have been different. But it's all too late . . .

What's the point? Well, death follows us around for a reason. It's because death is our best adviser. There is nothing more powerful than a person who is prepared to live right now, in this instant, fully accepting that this may be their last moment on earth.

If you're lost and looking for purpose, death can help. Sounds bizarre doesn't it? But bear with me. Most of us live our lives back to front. We look forward, always thinking there's plenty of time to do all the things we need to do. Then suddenly, like the deadline on a school assignment, death is right there in front of you and you have to cram to get it all done.

Try looking at things the other way around. Imagine the scene of your deathbed. Who is there? Who is not there? What are they saying about you? Now write your own eulogy. Sounds weird? Can't get in touch with it? Try going to a funeral and listening to the eulogies, I know this is pretty macabre but if it was so easy to work out your purpose in life someone would have given you an instruction book at birth. Just imagine it. "At the age of nineteen you will meet a lovely girl named Sally. You will be tempted to fall for her, but don't. She'll dump you for the captain of the football team. Go with Jenny instead, she's much more soulful."

Yeah right! How boring would life be? All those spontaneous moments ruined. "Wow, great idea, just hang on a sec and I'll check my instruction book to see if this is the right thing to do."

So, back to death. Embrace it, it's your friend and trustworthy adviser. It will help you work out what to do with those things you're passionate about.

Oh, and my friend who almost died?

She quit her job and decided to pursue what she was really passionate about. Now she is a top-class scuba

diving instructor and has a clarity of purpose that belies her youth. Is she afraid of death? No, because she's living her purpose now and it shines through in everything she does.

So don't wait until you are about to die before you start living. Embrace death and then consciously choose life.

My eulogy will read . . .

_____

_____

_____

_____

_____

_____

_____

_____

_____

_____

_____

_____

_____

NOTES

what will guide you?

A person's character is their destiny.
—Heraclitus

what's your price? Can you be bought? If so, are you cheap or expensive?

We admire heroes in movies who are willing to sacrifice themselves for their principles. You know the ones I mean—where the hero has been captured by the bad guys and they're torturing him or her to find out what they want to know. Does the hero give in? No way, they would rather endure pain than reveal their secret.

Nice idea, but what would you do in the same situation? What's your personal pain threshold that, if crossed, causes you to flee to the self? At what point do you say, stuff the rest of you. I'm looking after Number

One? There are a whole lot of TV shows on at the moment that reveal that for a little bit of cash most people will doublecross anyone. Just have a look at *Survivor*. When the contestants are together they're all chummy, but get them apart and they start saying things like, "I know it's bad to lie to them but we're playing for a million dollars here, it's not chicken feed."

Hmmm, too easy . . .

We need principles and values to guide us through life. Otherwise we're just like autumn leaves in the wind being blown all over the place. Values and principles keep us on track and provide an opportunity for the creation of trust. Not just trust in other people but, most importantly, trust in ourselves. If we know who we are and what we believe in, we provide ourselves with the freedom to explore relationships and grow in truth.

If we have no idea what we believe in, we'll go along with anything. Truth takes courage. Courage to stand up for what we believe in. Not necessarily in a confrontational way, but in a gentle yet firm way. Like an oak tree, able to sway gently in the wind, but strongly rooted into the ground.

If we know what we believe in, we have a stable base from which to explore other people's ideas and other cultures' values. From this base we can form deep and challenging friendships, founded on truth and trust. Integrity between our values and our actions gives us a strength of spirit that is evident to all who come in contact with us. Lack of integrity shows up just as quickly.

So, how do you work it out? How do you determine what values and principles are most important to you?

Start with a list. Think of all the people, real or fictional, that you admire, then write down why you admire them. For example, I admire Martin Luther King because he stood up for racial equality even when it was incredibly dangerous to do so. The character in *Gladiator*, Maximus, is admirable to me because he stands up for justice. Muhammad Ali gave up the heavyweight boxing title of the world for his right to choose his religious beliefs.

Once you have the list, identify what values or principles these people stood for that caused you to admire them. Values are generally just one word, but there are two different types. "Intrinsic values" have value in themselves. Examples include freedom, justice, honesty, and equality. "Instrumental values" have value through action. For example, productivity is a value but it has no value in itself, only through what it allows us to achieve by taking action.

The other point to note about values is that we don't see the values themselves, we only see the actions that reflect the values. For instance, if you believe that I'm an honest person it's not because I have "honest" tattooed on my forehead. Rather, because you have observed my

behavior over a period of time and have come to the con-
clusion that I act truthfully—that is, I'm honest. In this
way, values are like icebergs, most of them are hidden
below the surface. We have to guess what is there by
what we see above the surface.

People I admire   **Why?**

_____

_____

_____

_____

_____

_____

Key Values & Principles

_____

_____

_____

_____

_____

_____

_____

NOTES

talk is cheap

now you have a list of values you aspire to, but talk is cheap. You need to reflect on whether you have been living these values—do your deeds reflect your words?

One way of finding out is to look at the critical moments in your life where your values were tested. I mean, let's get serious here and cut the crap. A value is not a value unless you're willing to pay a price to uphold it. You can't say you believe in honesty and then tell lies all the time.

Just recently a new politician was elected to a seat formerly held by the opposition. At her inaugural press conference she said, "I pledge that I will work twelve hours a day, seven days a week, to represent the people in this electorate." A lie? I dont know, but it certainly sounds like an exaggeration to me. Personally, I'm immediately suspicious of anything that a politician says.

Critical moments are those times in your life when you're faced with a tough decision. Generally it's a choice between right and right when you are forced to take a stand. "Right and right?" Yes. "Right versus wrong" dilemmas such as, "Should I cheat on my golf scorecard?" are easy. It's the "right versus right" dilemmas that are difficult.

At these points we face a junction in the road of life. We must choose not only what values we support, but also show how strongly we believe in them by acting on them. Our actions reveal our character because character is action. Whatever choice you make at such moments will shape your life from that point forward and influence how you see yourself.

Consider young Andrew Jackman. At twelve years of age he finds himself in a very boring math class. Having just transferred from another school, he is sitting at the back of the classroom and is yet to find any new friends among his classmates. Billy Brown is a chubby, freckly-faced trouble-maker, and Andrew knows he is the ringleader of the class bad boys. Suddenly Billy throws a paper plane at the teacher, who is writing on the whiteboard. The pointy-nosed plane strikes Mr. Ross Farmer—a balding, cantankerous old man who is close to retirement—smack in the back of the head with a loud thwack.

He reels around, incensed by the stinging pain and, even more so, by the giggles of the students.

"Who threw that?" he demands.

Silence.

"I said, who threw that?"

Still silence.

"If someone doesn't own up immediately, you will all be in detention and a note will go on your records!"

As Ross Farmer scans the room with his steel-blue eyes, Andrew squirms in his seat, desperately trying to avoid eye contact.

Too late.

"Mister Jackman, you have a good vantage point there. You must have seen who threw it?"

Andrew looks up, the whole class is staring at him. Billy Brown glares at him threateningly from only a few inches away.

"Mister Jackman, I must assume that if you cannot name the culprit, then you are indeed he. In which case I will be forced to report this incident to the principal and have you suspended. Now, that's not a very nice way to start at a new school, is it?"

What should Andrew do? It would be right to tell the truth but then he would be an outcast. It would also be right to stick by the other students in the spirit of camaraderie.

What would you do? How will his choice shape his life

from that point on? What price should we be willing to pay to support certain values? How much is too much?

Or how about the situation where you are out having a drink at the local bar, and in walks your best friend with someone other than her boyfriend. She sees you and is embarrassed by the situation. You pull her to one side and ask what's going on. She explains that it's nothing, and begs you not to tell her boyfriend. The next day the boyfriend calls you and asks you to meet him for a coffee. Over coffee he tells you that he's suspicious of your best friend and asks you if you know whether anything is going on. To complicate matters, you've been interested in him for a while but haven't made a move because of your best friend.

What do you do?

Let's say you decide to be loyal to your friend and say nothing. A week later the boyfriend finds out. He's enraged. You go to console him (secretly hoping he'll get together with you) but he lashes out at you and calls you a bitch. A friend of his had seen not only his girlfriend and her new man at the bar but also you. Your chances with him are blown and now he's going about telling anyone who will listen that not only is your friend a tramp, but that you are a bitch. Your loyalty to your friend has cost you and will shape your life from that point on. Was it worth it?

The point is that we never understand the true significance of events as they occur. It is only when the present has become the past that events are rendered significant or empty. I could tell you now that Andrew Jackman decided not to tell the teacher who had thrown the jet plane and now he and Billy are best friends, albeit while sharing a cell at the Wentworth maximum security prison. Or that Andrew decided to tell and now he's the chief investigator for the tax department. Either way you might say, "I knew it!"

You see? We never know, we can't tell the future and we can't go back, all we have is the here and now. The only choice is to choose some key values and principles, and allow them to guide us so that we can look ourselves in the mirror at the end of the day. If we're just making it up as we go along it gets harder to keep track and eventually you lose the plot.

I'm not saying there's one way that's right and one way that's wrong. I'm saying you need to take the time to work out what's right for you. If you don't, you can be led astray by anyone.

I'm not saying you should become the moral policeman either. Let's face it, the Lord's Prayer doesn't say "Forgive us our sins" because it fits in neatly. It says it because we make mistakes every day so we need to be able to forgive each other but, most importantly, we need to be able to forgive ourselves. The concept of Karma works very well with Values. Be sure that if you go around judging everyone else for their failures then the harsh hand of judgment will slap you down on a regular basis. Be kind, that's what it's all about.

Failure to act in accordance with the things that we believe in also causes anger to arise within us. Action takes courage and courage only arises through strength of belief.

Consider a work situation where a group of people are taking a coffee break. Two women who have worked there for a long time complaining about a young girl who has just started. You listen to them, thinking how nasty they are being and how someone should tell them to back off. You care a bit more than most because you've been training the young girl and you know that she may be a little clumsy but she has good intentions. Suddenly she appears from behind the door, she's heard the whole thing. She looks at you with tears welling up in her eyes, then turns and walks away. You dash after her to console her but she'll have none of it, telling you instead that she feels betrayed and that she thought you, at least, would stick up for her.

You go home and look yourself in the mirror. All you can think is, "I should have said something."

Do you get the general idea?

Work out your Values and Principles. Then have a look, HONESTLY, at how you've been living and determine whether you've just been telling a good story or actually living what you preach. If you find that there's a big gap

between who you are being and who you aspire to be don't beat yourself up! Just gently acknowledge that you've got some work to do and recognize the lessons you've already learned.

the vision splendid

SO, let's pull all this together because it sounds easy so far . . .

First, be still. Life moves at such a fast pace these days that you have to create a discontinuance to change direction. There's a great line in an old Western movie when the two bandits have been on the run for a while out in the desert. They stop to take a break and one of them just wanders off into the scrub. "What are you doing?" the other one asks. "Sometimes you've just got to stop and take a look around," the bandit replies.

Ain't that the truth? Hustle and bustle, rush here and there, clock in, log out, check this, approve that . . . STOP! Take a deeeeeep breath and take a look around. Years ago I went overseas with a friend of mine. We wanted to backpack around the world but were both limited on time so we just crammed everything in. After four weeks of full-on traveling, I think we'd already visited seven or eight countries, we were standing in the Louvre in front of the *Mona Lisa*. We both looked at it, then looked at each other. "I thought it'd be bigger," my friend said. "Yeah," I replied, nonchalant. "What's next?"

We were numb to it, just as you can get numb to the routine of life. So, yes, stop, create a discontinuance in your life, take a look around, be still so you can let the silt settle in your mind.

Next is the passion thing. Make a list of possibilities. Like I said, you might not get it right away but at least you'll have a bundle of possibilities to get excited about. Forget about fear for the moment, that will only screw you up.

Now, death. This is key, it's time to live your life backward. Once you've written your eulogy, find a quiet place and start visualizing your ideal life.

Who is there? What type of people are they? How are they treating you? Where are you living? What type of place are you living in? What things do you have?

What are you doing? This will tie in with the passion question. There's a great story about a football coach who sat down when he was a young man and wrote a list of all the things he wanted to do before he died. He had 107 things on the list and by his midsixties he'd done 91 of them. Try it, you might be surprised by the result.

What are people saying about you? Do they think you're a slimy, two-faced charlatan they wouldn't touch with a ten-foot pole? Or are they speaking about you in revered tones?

Anyway, out of all of these things you need to create a Vision Splendid which you can see, feel, touch, smell, and hear. Elite athletes achieve amazing things because they practice them in their minds, over and over again. Life is the same. Be clear about what you want, practice it in your mind over and over again, and you will dramatically increase the chances of it coming out your way.

> Ask the world for great gifts and you
> encourage the world to deliver them to you.
> —Anon

If you can do this you're halfway to changing who you are being. A life lived with purpose is much more fulfilling than the emptiness that comes from just bouncing along from pillar to post.

The next thing is to make this Vision Splendid happen and to be happy along the journey.

My personal Vision is . . .

_____

_____

_____

_____

_____

_____

_____

_____

_____

_____

_____

_____

_____

_____

NOTES

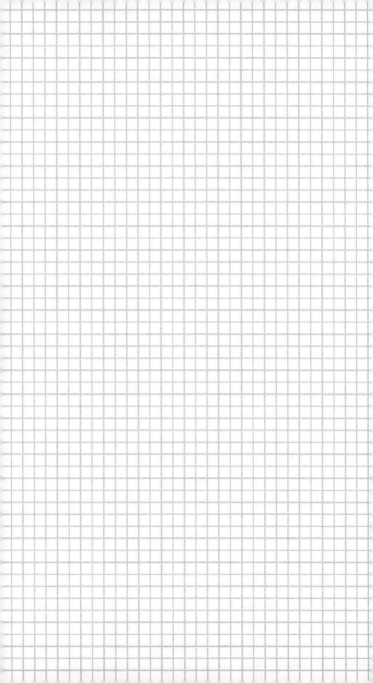

BE happy

happy?

what is happiness anyway? Mahatma Gandhi said, "Happiness is when what you think, what you say, and what you do are in harmony." The dictionary defines it as "contented with one's lot." But it is an elusive thing.

If you go around asking people if they are happy, most will shrug and reply "oh yeah" without ever really being sure. Happiness is a middle-of-the-road emotion. The only time we know for sure that we are happy is when we are joyful, and conversely, we know we are unhappy when we are sad. Happiness, or lack of it, is what's left over when nothing else is going on. Try it out. Go and sit in a room and do nothing, let everything settle, then check in. . . . Happy or unhappy?

So, are we born happy and have it taken away from us as we grow older? Or is it an unnatural state that we have to work toward? If you spend time with babies you'll soon realize that some of them are generally happy and others are downright grumpy. You'd think that happiness at that level could be fulfilled by satisfying some basic desires—you know, things like food and comfort. But it soon becomes obvious that even babies have bad days where they just can't be comforted.

Hell, even dogs have bad days. A friend of mine has an old, old pug named Milo. He has days where he's about as grumpy as an old man can get. Give him food, give him a pat, and speak to him nicely but he'll still just look up at you with weepy eyes as if to say, "Yeah, thanks, but I'm just having a shitty day, please leave me alone."

So, maybe happiness is an unnatural state that we have to work toward. If babies can have bad days and dogs can have bad days, how do they get over them? Surely it's just the allowance of time, the fulfillment of basic desires, and the mood passes? The problem is that as we grow older our list of "basic desires" grows longer. Instead of just needing food and physical comfort to be happy, we need the latest Nike shoes, the hippest, newest music, and the coolest clothes. And, on top of all that, we need recognition from our peers.

Before we know it, we have become slaves to our desires. We see unhappiness as an unnatural state of being, so as soon as we get into a less than happy mood we quickly try to cover it over. Avoid it at all costs, go out, see some friends, have a drink, take a pill and oops. . . . We're back on that road again.

Reminds me of a song by the The, which asks why God would be so cruel as to give us feelings that could never be fulfilled. The song concludes that true freedom is freedom from the heart's desire. Maybe that's the clue? Happiness is all about losing the self in the flow. We get thrown into the river of life at birth and we are swept along, caught in the current sometimes, trapped in eddies at others. All the while we desperately try to gain some degree of control. Try to clutch onto the reeds as they pass us by, not knowing that they will never be strong enough to hold us against the current for more than a moment. Then they break or we lose our grip and wheeeeee . . . Off we go again!

Maybe happiness is about letting go of the notion that things should be one way or another, and just accepting that they are, then letting go and enjoying the ride. Is this why drugs provide such attraction? I think so. When you're stoned or drunk you don't have concerns about the self because that is exactly what you're detached from. Conversely, when you're doing something you love, you've also lost touch with the concerns of the self. Escapism? Yes. But from what?

you

Hmmm . . . Get a grip! Life's an addiction, it's that darn monkey out of control again. It can be running rampant, jumping from tree to tree through the forest whacked out on drugs, or driven into a frenzy by retail therapy, or hyped up on sugar, or any other desire you care to name. In any case, the jar of water that is the rest of your mind is so stirred up by all the activity that you can't see anything and you have absolutely no idea what is going on at all.

Or . . . the monkey could be absorbed at a deep level by something you feel really passionate about. Then there is no need to try to control the monkey and no need to escape the self.

The moral of the story? Choose your addictions wisely.

Everyone has bad days. Don't believe anyone who tells you differently. It's just part of being human. The way we deal with them is the key. Some people put as much energy into being unhappy as they could into making themselves happy. Others resolve to get over it. The trick is to make a choice—do you want to be unhappy or happy? Now what are you going to do about it?

We shouldn't avoid unhappiness and we shouldn't believe that it's an unnatural state of being. We're feeling that way for a reason—we need to change something. Maybe we just need to change the way we are responding

BE

to a situation, maybe we need to change our job, our relationship, or our whole lives. Either way, the trick is choice, or freedom of choice to be precise. To be happy we have to feel that we are free to pursue the things we wish to pursue in life. Joy arises from following our passions, bitterness results from the lack of freedom. Happiness is about intention and believing that it's possible to change things.

If you want to be happy, the first thing you need to do is set your intention to be happy. Make a resolution now and stick it up on your wall—Be Happy.

be fit to fight

happiness. How badly do you want it? Are you willing to fight for it or do you think you can just sit back and expect the world to bring it to you on a platter?

If you want to lie down and feel sorry for yourself, go right ahead. There are plenty of people out there who are willing to join you on the carpet and plenty of others who will sell you things to assist you in your malaise. Drug-assisted living—don't imagine it's something new, it's been around since the beginning of time. Ever since people were conscious they have sought to escape from the pain of this reality and there are some who always will. Ancient peoples have used drugs as a way to open windows to other worlds and to glimpse unimagined realities. But when used simply as a means of escape, drugs are the easy way out. The way to lasting peace and happiness is a path that takes courage and the willingness to fight. To be able to fight, you've got to be fit.

Although sometimes we act as if our elements are separate, in reality they are tied together. Our mind, body, spirit, and emotions are interlinked like the four quarters of an apple. If we neglect one element and it begins to rot, the rot quickly spreads to the other parts, it can't be kept in isolation.

If you want to be emotionally fit to fight for happiness then you need to be fit physically, spiritually, and mentally as well. Go back and revisit your Vision. What image did you have of yourself? Were you fat and overweight or fit and healthy-looking? Lazy and lethargic or energetic and vibrant? Vague and dopey or sharp and on the ball?

Our minds can trick us into believing that in some way they are better than our bodies. There is even a saying that confirms this: mind over matter. But scientists have discovered recently that it works in reverse too. Matter influences mind. Just think about that for a second. In the past we've been told that if we are sad then all we have to do is convince ourselves that we are happy and bingo! Things change. Now they tell us that just by smiling we can trigger a "happy" response in our minds. Neat, heh?

So, those people who walk around with a smile perpetually glued to their faces might be onto something after all. If we look gloomy, we feel gloomy; if we feel gloomy, we

look even gloomier. . . . It's a vicious circle. Intent, remember that's the key. Intend to be happy, act happy, look happy, be happy, fight for it. . . .

Physical exercise is also important because it moves the energy. In a minute we'll look at movement and how important it is, but for the moment imagine that sadness and depression is a little man. He looks like a cartoon figure, he's short, maybe half a meter, has a pointy nose and wears a black hat and black coat. In his hands he carries a large black cape. I call this little man "Mel," short for Melancholy.

Mel visits me from time to time and I can sense when he's around because I tend to feel a bit low. When he visits, he follows me around the house waiting for me to stop so he can throw the black cape over me and plunge me into the darkness of depression. Luckily, he's not very tall so he needs me to stop and dwell on things. As soon as I do he pounces like a cat, throwing the cape, and down I go. Know the feeling?

Well the good part is that if you know when Mel is around, you can shake him off by moving the energy around you. Go for a walk, run, ride, whatever, and consciously shoo him away. How's a little man in a cape going to catch you on a bike? It works like a charm, try it!

We also need to be sharp mentally because fighting for happiness requires us to be on the ball. If we're not on the ball we can miss opportunities. They're called windows of opportunity for a reason; it's because if you don't jump through them fast enough they slam shut in your face.

I remember that when I left school, a good friend of my parents suggested I apply for a scholarship from a trust with which he'd been involved so that I could go to England and study. I was pretty cocky and figured that if he'd asked me then it was a given—something that was there for the taking any time I felt like it. Well, what a stupid young smart ass I turned out to be. When I finally got around to it, the application period had closed. I'd missed the opportunity and there were no second chances.

Research into the brain shows that the mind is just like the muscles in your body. It needs to be exercised to stay fit and healthy. If you don't exercise it, then it withers away. If you do exercise it but only in a limited way, it becomes stiff and rigid, unable to do new things. Mind work needs to be varied, challenging, and fun. There's no point just grinding deeper and deeper ruts into the mind. Try doing a variety of things. Dance, learn a language, play chess, play a musical instrument, read, whatever . . . just make it varied and challenging.

Spirit is the last area that needs exercise. It's the thing that is intangible yet has the power to lift you above and beyond what you could ever rationally believe to be possible.

The third part of this book deals with spirit in more depth so I'll leave it till then and move on, instead, to Choice.

fate versus freedom

lots of people say that life is predetermined, so what is the point of trying to change anything? Let's first consider this, assuming that there is no God, higher being, or higher consciousness. Remember that this presumes that there is no purpose to life either, because there is no creative force.

If that is the case then everything we do and everything that happens to us has been predetermined. So, no matter what we do it won't change anything. Shit will happen anyway.

If this is true then life truly is suffering. We can be no more than pawns at the mercy of our desires, alternating between the joy arising from the fulfillment of our desires and the pain experienced in being unable to fulfill them.

If you believe this then you may as well pursue pleasure at every turn because nothing you do will change the outcome of your life.

To me, this is a cop-out because you're refusing to take responsibility for anything that happens to you, or anything you do. "It's just fate" is the catch-cry of people who believe this. This view on life absolves you from responsibility but provides you with no true freedom because you must believe that your hands were tied at birth.

If you believe this view of the world you may as well stop reading now because there is no point trying to change anything in your life or in your world.

By the way, if you've guessed that view of life irritates me you're on the money. "Go away and put your head back in the sand" is what I say to these people (with love and compassion, of course). "You're just a passenger. . . ."

Anyway, back to fate. So, now let's assume that you believe in God or a God-like presence. I should clarify this because many people have a great aversion to the term God, because of the idea of a male God sitting up on high looking down upon us with judgment in his heart. No, when I refer to God, I am referring to the notion of a creative force or higher power that pervades all things.

The Bantu people in Africa believe that God rules in the present, the past, and the future, but that God can not be comprehended. Christians believe that we are created in God's image and have generally used a male figure to depict God. Other religions believe that God is everything and everywhere. Various spiritual teachings believe that there is a universal life force that pervades all things. Whatever works for you is what I say. But generally the question is, "Is there a higher power or not?" For ease, I'll call this God, but please don't get triggered by this. As I said, fit whatever image to this that suits you.

Oh yes, fate . . .

Okay, so let's assume there is a God. If everything is predetermined and there is no freedom of choice then God has created a world where we are just pawns. God created us and put us in this world but he already knows what will happen to us. No matter how hard we struggle we can't change a thing. All the pain, suffering, struggle, etc., etc. are for nought. The only one who would get any amusement out of this would be God—sounds very cruel to me and totally at odds with the idea of God anyway.

A loving, benevolent God who would create a world where our most basic freedom is taken away is an oxymoron. On that basis, I reject the concept.

If there is a God who is loving, benevolent, and kind, then surely God would create a world in which we have freedom of choice. The power to change things.

Now, obviously we can't change the circumstances of our lives. We can't change our parents or where we were born. But we can change the conditions. We can decide to remain in the gutter or to haul ourselves out. We can change how we react to what goes on around us.

Ever seen the movie *Groundhog Day*?

If not, go rent it. Bill Murray is the lead and he experiences the same day over and over again, until he realizes that all he has to do is change the way he is reacting to the events of the day. Life's much the same.

A point to note here though. If we are brainwashed from an early age to believe that we are losers, then every time something bad happens to us we'll say, "That's right, I'm a loser" and reinforce the belief. So, although we CAN change things it doesn't mean that it is easy to do, especially if you're already carrying around a huge amount of baggage about who you are. Which brings me to my next point.

belief creates reality

I don't have to be who you want me to be.
—Muhammad Ali

if we are created in God's image, then ALL of us are, not just some of us. If some of us can do amazing things then ALL of us can do amazing things. In essence, YOU ARE WHAT YOU BELIEVE.

What screws us up are the crazy ideas put into our heads and the things society wants us to believe so that we fit in. Society wants us to believe that we must get a job and fit into the economic system so that we can buy things and be happy. The people dominating the world would have us believe that everything's hunky dory.

At present we're in a really weird place. In the 1970s we were all talking about the "Golden Age of Leisure" that was just around the corner. The working week was getting shorter and things were looking good. People expected that before too long the average working week would be four days and they would have more time to spend with their family or pursuing other things.

what's happened?

The average working week has gotten longer, people are now more stressed than ever, parents are spending less and less time with their kids, and it's almost impossible for the average person to support a family on one income. On top of all this, there is increasing evidence that the planet's resources are being plundered and our grandkids will inherit a wasteland.

Hello? Is anybody listening? Ever get the impression that maybe we're heading in the wrong direction? It's no wonder there's an increase in depression! If you look objectively at how things are going, how can you not be depressed?

But it doesn't have to be this way!! If we keep going the way we are then we'll end up just where we're headed. Big change is needed, faith in a different direction is key. Most importantly, we need to reclaim our freedom. Our freedom to choose who we are and what sort of world we want to create. As long as we continue to just react to what's going on around us, we'll never be free.

BE

> There is nothing either good or bad,
> but thinking makes it so.
> —*Hamlet*, Shakespeare

Our beliefs create our reality. If we believe we're stupid then we are stupid, we don't even attempt complex things because we know we can't do them. If we believe in fate then we resign ourselves to fate and don't even bother fighting to change things. If we believe we are a great tennis player then we can be a great tennis player. It doesn't mean we will be but it does open up the possibility. Consider the reverse—if we believe we are a crap tennis player then we most definitely will never be a good one.

Of late, quantum physics has been catching up with some of this stuff. The Heisenberg principle states that an object is affected by its interaction with a subject. Our thoughts are things. In other words—and they've tested this—if you stare at someone, they will be affected by your staring. Some people can tell when they are being looked at with about ninety percent accuracy.

The power of collective belief is huge. Clarity of intent can have a huge impact when backed by belief. Note also that everything affects everything else. What you believe affects what you think. The way you think affects the way you talk. The way you talk affects the way you are perceived. The way you are perceived affects the way you are treated. The way you are treated affects what you believe.

If you believe you are a winner you act like a winner. If you act like a winner you walk and talk like a winner. You get treated like a winner. Mind over matter. Belief and intent equals creation. Just check out Andre Agassi next time he's playing a close tennis match.

The trick is to unmask our illusions. To dig so deep into our own psyche that we can determine what it is that we believe at a deep level. Are we being supported or undermined by our subconscious? Are we self-sabotaging or self-supporting?

I've noted before that our western society is built on linear type thinking, which can be traced all the way back to the Greek philosophers—Socrates, Plato, and Aristotle. But there is another way of looking at the world. One that is much more fluid and much more aligned to the power of creative manifestation.

If we look at the world as a place where energy flows through things, and accept that our thoughts and beliefs affect things, then the world becomes infinitely creative in every minute of every day.

Let's divide the world into three domains: Past, Present, and Future.

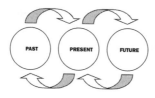

In the past we have all of our experiences, beliefs, opinions, and judgments. In short, all of the things that make us who we are. We drag all of those things into the present because when faced with a situation in the present, our first point of reference is the past.

For example, if we have been told in the past that we are not attractive, when faced with a potential sexual encounter in the present we will act in accordance with our beliefs. Most likely we will create the outcome we expect.

This might sound all too simple to you because we like to believe that as humans we are incredibly complex and unique beings. But that is exactly why we form patterns in our minds. Even the simplest of tasks can be done in a myriad ways. If we had to consider all of the possibilities in life before making a decision, we would be paralyzed by indecision. Just putting on our clothes in the morning would take us hours.

Scientists recognized a long time ago that our minds free us from this analysis by operating as a self-organizing patterning system. Sounds complex, eh? But it isn't. All it means is that our mind is constantly looking for patterns in the things we see and do. As soon as it sees a pattern, it shifts into automatic mode and follows the pattern rather than considering the other possibilities.

Consider this analogy that Dr. Edward De Bono uses. Imagine a flat desert plain where rain begins to fall. Slowly, puddles will form. As more rain falls, some of the puddles will join together, then the water will start flowing from the highest to the lowest point. As the water flows it will form streams that will get deeper and deeper as more water flows through them. The next time it rains the water will flow directly into these streams and they will get deeper, possibly forming rivers.

On and on the process will go, all the while becoming more and more automated.

The same thing happens in our minds. For instance, we are sleep-trained as babies. We start off waking up several times during the night and eventually, to our parents' joy, we sleep through the night. Some of us even get put to sleep by being driven around in a car, then we wonder why some people fall asleep at the wheel in later life. Ironic, eh?

The point is that many things are preprogrammed into our minds, forming patterns that we follow without even thinking.

If our mind is full of getting it wrong then it's pretty hard to get it right. Our past makes up our fixed view of the world and dictates how we perceive the world. Without exception, we will act in accordance with our perceptions. Our past will limit our perceptions, restricting the way we deal with situations in the present to just a series of options, not the true range of possibilities.

Most people live their lives ninety to ninety-five percent in the past/present loop. Because they know what the world is, they get exactly what they expect. The more they go around and around the loop, the deeper the ruts in their minds get and the harder it is to break out of the cycle.

From birth we are brainwashed into believing that this cycle is the best way to go. We can make incremental improvements to our lives, but large-scale change escapes us.

The world is like this at the moment—stuck in a short-sighted capitalist loop that is spinning in ever-decreasing circles. Most people are acting just like the passengers they are. Going along for the ride, having no idea where the journey will end, but staying onboard just the same. Safe and secure but going nowhere.

I'll say it again. No wonder so many people are depressed and suicidal.

breaking out of
the loop

sometimes we get out of the
loop by accident. We get so angry with the way things are
that we decide we're not going down the same old road
again. We rule out what's worked in the past and decide
to start with a blank sheet of paper.

This is when we're moving over into that future
domain. In the future, anything is possible, we truly start
with a blank sheet and nothing constrains us.

The problem is that when we go over to the future, come
up with some new ideas, and then come back to the present to tell people, they try to drag us back into the past.
Remember that the past is safe, secure, relaxed, and, most
importantly, supported by everyone else around you. They'll
tell you it can't be done and back it up with lots of evidence
from the past. If you do attempt to do something, the first

time something goes wrong there'll be a chorus of people telling you they told you so.

Tell them to Go Away! No, not really, only kidding . . . Recognize instead that everybody has dreams, but not many people have the courage to pursue them. Dead dreams rot within us. Not being able to do what we want causes bitterness. Bitterness manifests as anger, jealousy, or depression. So don't be surprised if people get confrontational and tell you why you can't do things. They're just reflecting their fixed view of the world.

Anyway, back to getting out of the loop. If we are going to shift our way of being from the past/present loop into the future/present loop, we need some new anchor points. In the past/present loop our anchor points for behavior are all the things that we know to be right through experience and upbringing. There is lots of support for these things in society because we're all brainwashed pretty uniformly.

BE

the three domains of communication

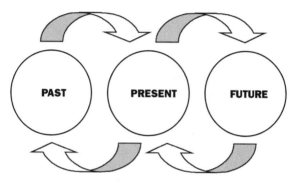

- ■ Fixed view of the world
- ■ Comfortable and safe
- ■ We know everything
- ■ The total of our experiences, opinions, judgments
- ■ Right/Wrong
- ■ Offers only options, not true possibilities

- ■ What is or is not
- ■ The present is the place where spirit and matter connect and hence is your point of power where you have an opportunity to influence the world
- ■ The only place where actions happen

- ■ The opportunity to explore true possibilities
- ■ A blank canvas

Once you step over into the future/present loop you're stepping into a void. The reference points from the past/present loop are no longer valid. In fact, as I've already mentioned, they will invalidate what you are trying to do.

So you need some new reference points, or anchor points, to cling to as you go through the storm. These anchor points are: your Vision Splendid; your Values; and your plan of Action.

The first part of this book detailed how to determine your Vision and your Values. We'll deal with Actions in a minute. First let's go back and look at this view of the world in more detail.

On their own, the past and the future are just talk fests—nothing happens in the past and the future. The only place where things happen is the present. However, the past can hold us back through the power of belief and the future can propel us forward through clarity of Intent.

So, first we need to find out—what's holding you back?

clearing a space in the clutter of the mind

the way the world works is that like attracts like, so if you put worried thoughts about what might happen to you out into the world then you increase the chances of these things happening. Basically we manifest whatever we put out. So you'd better work out what your mind is full of right now, then decide which part of it is useful and which part isn't. Throw out the useless parts and make some room for the new. If your mind is full of rubbish, no matter how hard you try to take in new things you will fail because there is no space.

Imagine that your mind is like the fixed memory capacity on a computer. Once it is full, the whole system grinds to a halt because everything is crammed in so tight that nothing can move. If confusion reigns in our minds then confusion will reign in our world. Time to purge.

The first trick is to write down everything you know to be true about yourself. How do you know it's true? Because everyone else has told you it is. Try it this way.

My mom says:
    "You're just like your dad, you're too impatient, you don't tolerate fools."
My girlfriend says:
    "You're easy to talk to, you're fun to be around."

This list might take you a while to complete as it's useful if you can go through all of the significant people in your life. . . .

Once you have the list, go through it and work out which ones are useful and which ones aren't. By useful, I mean consider the type of person you need to be to achieve your Vision Splendid. What behaviors or character traits fit?

For the judgments that aren't useful, acknowledge that they aren't useful and decide what you're going to do to change them. This could mean you are going to change your behavior, or it could mean that you are going to speak to that person every time they pass that particular judgment on you.

Remember, you are what you believe. So if someone you care about is continually saying something to you in a judgmental way that is not useful, it is bound to have a negative effect on you. If they care about you and what you are trying to achieve, then it should just be a matter of pointing out to them what effect their words are having on you.

For instance imagine that every time you lose your temper your mother, without really thinking about it, says to you, "You're just like your father." Imagine too that your father has a bad temper that he has trouble controlling. A temper that has cost him several jobs and career opportunities, limiting him to an unfulfilling job when he has the potential to be much more. Not only will you interpret your mother's comments as being negative, you may also see your temper as something that is beyond your control.

Don't buy into it!

True power is the ability to proactively determine your response to any situation.

You can be whoever you want to be, you are only limited by your beliefs. Instead of simply reacting to what your mother has said, calmly (maybe walk away and come back later if you're really pissed off) point out to her that her comments are very negative and her judgment gives you nowhere to move, gives you no opportunity to change, and that you would like her support in changing yourself for the better.

This may sound a bit trite but it does work. At the very least, pointing out to other people the effect their words have will cause them to stop and reflect on how they are behaving.

What people say about me   **Useful?**
                                      Yes/No

_____

_____

_____

_____

_____

What I'm going to do about it

_____

_____

_____

_____

_____

_____

_____

NOTES

Next, sit down quietly and write out a description of how you see yourself. You've got to be brutally honest! What are your negative points or weaknesses? What are your strengths?

Then do the same exercise as before. Identify which ones are useful and which ones aren't, and determine what action you are going to take on the negative points.

How I see myself

Useful?
Yes/No

_____

_____

_____

_____

_____

What I'm going to do about it

_____

_____

_____

_____

_____

_____

_____

_____

NOTES

At the end of this exercise you will have a long list of things to do or to change. You should also be getting a more clearer picture of who you are trying to be.

Now during your meditations you should be able to listen to the chatter in your mind and decide if it is reflecting who you want to be, or who you don't want to be.

acts have power

hopefully, by now you're getting a good idea of how this way of looking at the world works. Talk is cheap, acts have power. The present is your point of power, it's the only place where spirit and matter meet, the only place where you have an opportunity to interact with the material world.

Change your beliefs and you change the vibe you put out into the world. Change your Vision and you change what you intend to create. But, and this is a big But, nothing happens without ACTION.

One cannot learn wisdom by sitting at another's feet. One must live one's own life, make one's own mistakes, feel one's own ecstasy to learn the true meaning of existence, for it is different in each

individual. Fall down, get up, do it all over again in
another context.
Experience. And learn. That's the only way.
—*The Ninja*, Eric Van Lustbader

If you are in the past/present loop then you are merely reacting to everything that happens around you. Your actions are perpetuating the way things have always been. If you're in the future/present loop you need to be proactive. Don't wait. Never wait for things to happen. As soon as you wait you have lost control of the situation, you will only be reacting.

The future/present loop is all about creative manifestation. It's about deciding on what it is you want to create, then going out there and doing it. Even if the world tells you that you can't.

They did it in the United States in the late 1960s when they decided to put a man on the moon. Lots of eminent scientists said it couldn't be done. Instead of arguing with them, Kennedy put them in a building together and asked them to determine exactly why it couldn't be done. He then took their answers and gave them to another group of scientists. They found the solutions to the problems. At first they could only get a man halfway back to earth but by the end . . . well, you know the end.

So, this is a key point. The old way of looking at the world

BE

is very fixed. Socrates, Plato, and Aristotle, and the thinking that goes with them, were all for defining the world and putting things into categories and boxes. Deciding what is right and what is wrong.

This new way of looking at the world is all about movement. Creation assumes that the world is a mystery, that there is no definitive right answer. It also accepts that the world is infinitely abundant, whereas the old way assumed that the world is scarce. Instead of deciding how to divide up the cake amongst competing needs, we need to work out how to make a bigger cake.

Get clarity of Vision, have Belief, set your Intention and CREATE!

ACT!

> Concerning all acts of initiative (and creation) there is one elementary truth, the ignorance of which kills countless ideas and splendid plans: that the moment one definitely commits oneself, then Providence moves too. All sorts of things occur that would never otherwise have occurred. A whole stream of events issues from the decision, raising in one's favor all manner of unforeseen incidents and meetings and material assistance, which no (human) could have dreamed would have come his way.
>
> —Goethe

You can't create movement by thinking about things (unless you can bend spoons with your mind). You need to act.

Once you have belief in what you are trying to create, work out exactly what acts will be perfectly aligned to the creation of that reality. In other words, believe that your Vision exists at some point in the future. All you have to do is draw it toward you. If you can see the path that leads to that Vision, then what acts are on that path? What are the significant milestones along the way? What do you need to do right now? What do you need to have done within six months? What do you need to have done within a year?

Acts on the path to my Vision

_____

_____

_____

My Milestones

_____

_____

_____

What I need to do within the next six months

_____

_____

_____

What I need to do right NOW

_____

_____

_____

_____

NOTES

the space invaders
strategy for life

ever play the video game Space Invaders?

As a teenager I spent hours and hours hanging out in arcades playing video games . . . and trying to look cool and pick up girls of course!

Space Invaders was the really popular game—not just because we worked out that we could get free games by zapping the coin slot with an electronic lighter! But because it required real skill, luck, and strategy.

To be an ace Space Invaders player required not only an understanding of the strategy, but the nerve to carry it out—and here's the relevance.

You see, in the game, row upon row of little invaders advance upon your position. The temptation is to shoot at them randomly but if you adopt this strategy you get quickly overrun.

BE

To get a really high score, you need to shoot out a couple of columns and then calmly and methodically shoot out one row at a time. If you hold your nerve and just concentrate on the moment, even when you are about to be overrun, the strategy works. But if you panic, you are doomed.

Life is just the same—you need a strategy to get to where you want to be. But then the real skill is having the nerve to carry it out. Be completely present, just concentrate on shooting the invaders next in line or on doing the next few actions that are required. Don't panic when the people looking over your shoulder say you're about to be killed. Be on the ball during each offensive and take stock between "games."

don't be paralyzed

perched on the precipice of the future, it is easy to become paralyzed by analysis. But come back to your trusted adviser, death. If not now, then when? Remember, nothing is more powerful than a person who acts as if this is his last act on this earth.

Once you have a plan of action then get on with it. Remember, you can't know the future and you can't understand the true implications of what is happening now until it's too late anyway. Whatever decisions you make, make them one hundred percent, don't live life in half measures.

Fear never bites as hard as regret.

Worry is a pointless emotion because we are being triggered by something that hasn't happened. It causes us to cling desperately to the world, and this depletes not only ourselves but also the world. Whatever is going to happen in the future will happen in the future. The only opportunity you have is right now, right in front of you.

I know that it's easy to say "don't worry" but it's often much harder to do. If you're a perpetual worrier, and you'd like to be different, then you need to do some digging. Not in the backyard but in your mind. What's happened in your life to create the pattern that makes you worry?

If you can uncover what these things are, then you have a much better chance of doing something about them. Maybe it's just a matter of acknowledging the point-lessness of worrying about things and resolving to be different. Maybe you need to take some action to clear the behavior pattern. Either way, you need to determine how it is you want to be. And start acting in alignment with that vision.

when things don't go right

The real challenge in life
is to always look forward.
—John Travolta

okay, so I need to come clean. . . . Things won't always go your way. Yes, I know it's hard to believe, but it's true. In any case, you need to have a plan to deal with things when they don't turn out the way you want.

First, let's have a look back at that model. If you try something you've never done before and it doesn't work out, the first thing that will happen is that you will go straight back into the past. Immediately you will have a big story, all about how you knew you shouldn't have done it, tried it, or believed it. About what a fool you were to believe that you could have done it in the first place. About how you should have listened to all the people who said you couldn't do it . . .

STOP!

Now, here's the tricky bit. You need to work out what part of your babble is the story and what parts are the facts. There is a difference, although we do tend to confuse them on a regular basis. The facts are what cannot be disputed. Facts either are, or they aren't—simple, no debate.

The story is all the rest of the babble, all of the opinion about who was right, who was wrong, who knew you shouldn't have done it, who told you so. . . .

Ahhh! Again, get it clear, write it down, work it out. What are the facts? What actually happened? What do you want?

Consider this example. A young friend of mine, Matt, is a potter. He was working in the United States when he heard about a pottery in the mountains of South Africa that took on apprentices. He tracked down the owner of the pottery and over a period of time convinced her to let him go down there for six months. So, he packed his bags and headed down there, expecting to find a large, modern pottery with a semiattached apartment for his own use.

When he got there, he found that the pottery was an old converted stable with ancient equipment. The apartment

was the last stable in the building, with a wall in the middle to divide it into a bedroom and a kitchen with the small bathroom off to one side.

The pottery wheel he was given wasn't even balanced, so every time he tried to throw a pot it was lopsided. The apartment had flow-through ventilation that was great for keeping cool but let all the bugs in, and the hot water was nonexistent.

After a few days he was in quite a state. He would tell anyone who cared to listen what a terrible predicament he was in.

Finally, we went through the past/present/future way of looking at the world together. He immediately saw what was going on. He had a really long story to tell but the facts were simple: the pottery wheel was out of balance, there was no hot water and the apartment let the bugs in.

Slowly, he gained some objectivity. Instead of being ruled by his emotions and just reacting to the situation he was in, he asked, "What do I want?"

He knew that what he wanted was to spend some time living and working in another culture, so that he could grow as a person and develop his pottery skills. His Vision was clear.

The next question was, "Are you still committed to the Vision?" To which he answered a resounding "Yes!"

So then his back was up, worry was gone, he was ready for action. "So, what's next?" I asked.

He jumped to his feet, and as he walked up the hill to the pottery he called back to me, "Fix the wheel, get someone to fix the hot water, plug up the holes in the apartment, and get on with it."

We all fall down from time to time and, as I've mentioned earlier, if there is one skill in life that we all need to learn it's how to get back up, dust ourselves off, and get on with things. The keys are the willingness to do it and the process that gives us access to it.

> The greatest glory in living lies not in
> never falling down but in rising each
> time we fall.
> —Nelson Mandela

If we try to achieve great things, to pursue our dreams no matter how crazy they may seem to others, then we need to accept that we will fall down more often than if we simply get on the train and go along for the ride.

Remember, true power is the ability to proactively determine your response to any situation, and creation comes about through movement. So, we must be clear on what we are trying to achieve, be objective enough to pull ourselves out of the mire and be willing to keep moving.

The next time you go off the rails, stop and ask yourself these questions:

- What actually happened? Not the story, just the facts.

- What do I want?

- Do I still want it?

- What action is next?

Then just do it! Yes, I know, terribly clichéd, but Nike did get one thing right.

Remember also that there is still a use for the past/present loop. Don't throw the baby out with the bathwater. While the future/present loop allows us to manifest or create things, the past/present loop is the loop of continuous improvement. So, from a factual perspective, we can ask, "Is there anything I can learn from that experience to help me next time?"

Matt learned that when you're trying to do something that is a bit of a stretch, it's useful to have someone there to help you through the times when things aren't going your way. I know from my personal experience that when things go bad I tend to sit around and mope and feel sorry for myself. I like to tell people how bad things are and how unjust the world is. But I have someone I call who I know will give me some sympathy, but then give me a good kick in the ass to get me back into action.

So, here are some more ideas:

- Ask someone you trust to help you achieve what you're trying to do. Essentially they will be your coach and they must be clear about this role when you need their help. Make sure they are as committed to achieving your goals as you are.

- Get really good at recognizing when you are becoming reactive and need help. Sometimes it might feel good to suffer on your own but it won't get you anywhere fast. Recognize it, call it, ask for help.

don't flog
a dead horse

If you're selling water in the desert and
it rains you stop selling water and start
selling umbrellas.
—Anon

as good as your plan is, it might be the wrong one.

Damn!

Yes, I know, how could that be so?

Well that's the beauty of life, isn't it? We don't know what's going to happen next. Something might be right at one point in time, but a few months down the track it becomes wrong. You've got to be able to recognize the difference between facing obstacles and challenges, and actually being on completely the wrong track.

When trading futures the first rule is, "Be prepared to cut your losses." But, no matter how many times people get told that, they still become emotionally attached to the decisions they've made and refuse to sell a losing position. As the stock is going down and they're losing their house they'll say, "Don't worry, the market's going to turn around any second now." Maybe, maybe not.

When pursuing big goals in life you need to be able to hold onto them lightly. There may be a better way, but if you hold onto one goal really tightly you'll never see the alternatives.

How do you know?

I think we get given clues along the way. The challenge is to be able to recognize them. Consider this example. I was the director of a small company that was about to reposition itself in the market. To do this, I decided we needed to get some new stationery printed. So I commissioned a graphic artist to put something together.

From day one, nothing went right. Files got lost, communications were misunderstood, money transfers went astray, the list went on. But, pigheaded as I am, I persisted and finally the new design was approved and sent off to the printer.

In the week between the designs being approved and the cards being received, two things happened. A large client approached us to do some work that was slightly outside of what we'd been doing, and several people gave us feedback that indicated a change of name was in order.

The result? The company name was immediately changed, making the new cards redundant the day they arrived from the printer. In retrospect, there were lots of clues to indicate that I was on the wrong track. But I was just too pigheaded to listen.

So, be firm and determined but don't be so emotionally attached to being right that you ignore the warning signs.

dealing with
difficult people

Treat a man as he is and he will remain as he is.
Treat a man as he can and should be and he will become
as he can and should be.
—Goethe

ah yes, you may have come across some difficult
people during the journey. They're the ones who always
seem to be trying to throw you off track. Do you know the
type of people I mean? The ones who disturb your balance and maybe drive you to the brink of insanity.

Let me explain. . . .

I shared a house with a girl named Kathy. I was
responsible for paying the rent on time, and she was supposed to deposit her rent into my account. Something
she never, in six months of living together, did on time. We
each bought food for the house but she invariably drank

all the beer and didn't buy more. I used to travel for work at the time and I'd go away for a week and return to a house bereft of food or drink. When I confronted her about any of these issues she immediately became reactive and started telling me that I was bossing her around and not allowing her to feel at home in the house.

It's a neat trick, huh? If I went ballistic at her then I would be doing exactly what she said I was doing and would immediately make her the victim. If I ignored all the things she was doing then I felt I was being used and would get more and more frustrated by the situation.

There are lots of people like this around. They are very good at suckering you into their view of the world and once they've got you where they want you, it's very hard to get away. The key is to recognize that you're being set up to react a certain way. Remember, true power is being able to determine your response to any situation. As soon as you react, you're out of control.

Kathy had a boyfriend, Gareth. One time I went away for a week and returned to find a note that said, "Don't freak out but Gareth has moved in for a few days."

Don't freak out? Why shouldn't I freak out? I go away for a few days and you move someone else into the house? Ever heard of cell phones? Ever think to call me?

And there it is—the setup. The note should have read, "I dare you to freak out because then you'll be the asshole and Gareth will be the victim."

Difficult people have a view of the world that they want you to support. They lay traps for you and tempt you to fall into them. Then they are in control and their behavior will be excused.

Now, don't get me wrong. Usually difficult people aren't being malicious. They've just set up their lives so that they can be excused for living the way that they do, because the world is unjust and they are the victims. They are effectively running a racket in their mind that absolves them from trying to do what they really want in life. The problem is that they need a continual flow of evidence to support this view of the world, so they set situations up. And that's where you and I come in. . . .

Let's go back to Gareth. Pretty soon he's made himself at home and starts treating the place as a hotel. He comes and goes as he pleases, generally only stopping to eat whatever food is in the fridge.

After a couple of weeks enough is enough and I tell him he's got to find somewhere else to live. So, can you guess his reaction? That's right! He rants and raves about what an asshole I am and how unfair I'm being, never considering for a second how fortunate he has been to stay in the house in the first place. In his view of the world he is a victim and the world is unjust so he's just acting accordingly. He goes to his friends and tells them how badly he's been treated. Voilà, he has their sympathy. "Oh you poor thing how could anyone be so cruel to you. . . ."

This view of the world allows Gareth to say to himself things like, "If only the world wasn't so unfair then I could do all the things I want to do." The racket releases Gareth from ever having to make an attempt at life.

How to deal with people like this?

Confront difficult people with kindness and truth. Recognize that in life you can't always be the good guy in the eyes of others. You have to be able to make hard decisions and the only way you can do this is if you know what you believe in and you have the trust in yourself to carry it through. Not in a nasty way but in a firm but gentle way, based on truth.

Refuse to play the game, refuse to be manipulated, refuse to relinquish control and become reactive, have the courage of your convictions and maintain your course. If you refuse to play the game and refuse to be an asshole, then their attention will have to turn to themselves and this is the last thing they want.

If you have the strength of will to hang in there and not react, then very quickly these people will move away from you and find someone else who will play their game.

pay the price?

there are some people for whom life seems to come really easily. Put it down to past-life karma I say, and get over it. For the rest of us, pursuing dreams can be a struggle and there is often a price to pay.

Sometimes that price is too high and other times we just make excuses so that we don't have to pay the price. Our mind plays tricks on us, the monkey wants to control us, and most of us fall for it more often than not.

Years ago, I wanted to write a movie screenplay but I was afraid that it would be terrible. I wasn't willing to admit that I was afraid, so I used to say to myself that I'd start writing as soon as I had enough money so I could stop working for a while. Naturally, that was never going to happen because although one part of me wanted to start writing, another part, the monkey that was having fun swinging around the jungle, had no intention of ever letting me do it.

Part of creating something new is being able to uncover the excuses that we make in our minds. I like to ask corporate executives how many hours a week they work. Usually they say fifty or sixty. I then ask how many hours they'd like to work, and they say thirty or forty. Why they don't do it is the obvious question. The most common reason is that it's the way of business these days, so they believe they have to work that much. Who decides that? It's just the general consensus of the executives themselves, and it's driven by fear. Fear that if they work less they won't fit in. Fear that if they work less they will be left behind. Fear that if they work less someone else will take their job.

Sure, if you want to work long hours, go ahead. But if you don't want to, then don't. Don't be driven by fear, be driven by intent. But, and this is a big But, be aware that there is a price and be willing to pay it. Don't expect others to pay it for you. Take full responsibility.

Recognize too that the longer you have been doing something, the deeper the ruts are, and the harder it is to break out of the pattern.

With any behavior, there's a price and a payoff. Be clear what they are, know what you want and be prepared to enlist someone to help you create a new path in your life.

seize the gift

Sweet are the uses of adversity which
like the toad ugly and venomous wears
yet a precious jewel in his head.
— *As You Like It*, Shakespeare

every challenge we are presented with also
provides an opportunity to seize a gift of power. Sounds
mysterious, eh?

Every time you face a challenge in your life, you are
being tested as to how strong your beliefs and intentions
are. Each time you are being asked if you have the
courage to stand by those beliefs. If you stand up for
what you believe in and face the challenge head-on then
you come out the other side with a renewed belief in the
validity of your intentions.

We admire people who go through great hardship to achieve greatness. They have a kind of aura about them that says, "Don't mess with me, I know what I'm about. I have been thoroughly tested in battle."

The challenges you face in your life are the same. Confront them with a brave face. The greater the challenge the greater the gift of power.

I used to be terrified of emotionally charged women. I just didn't know how to deal with them, so I avoided confrontations with women I knew would fly off the handle easily. Anyway, the universe must have decided that it was time for me to face this issue. I started being confronted over and over again by situations in which a woman was being emotional.

I had the whole range. My mom got upset about something that happened and cried. My girlfriend got upset with me and yelled and cried. A woman I worked with got furiously angry with me, and a female friend went through a deep depression.

At first I had no power over my reactions at all and I was unable to say what I wanted to say—I just wanted to escape the situations as soon as possible. But slowly, as I faced each situation and worked my way through it, I began to find my feet and stopped just reacting. Slowly I was able to seize the gift of power.

The day I knew I had it under control was when I was sitting in my most emotionally charged female friend's swimming pool and the filter began to act up. Having everyone as a handyman, I decided I'd try to fix it and confidently started turning taps and adjusting things. Suddenly, with my friend looking over my shoulder, the filter pump made a kind of groaning sound and then with an almighty bang, one of the pipes burst open and we were standing under a fountain of water.

I looked at my friend, momentarily terrified of her reaction, and then burst out laughing. She soon joined in and ever since I've cherished the gift.

Other situations provide us with opportunities to receive different types of gifts, but they all have one thing in common—the requirement of courage.

get serious

It is not the critic who counts, not the one who
points out how the strong man stumbled or how
the doer of deeds might have done them better.
The credit belongs to the man who is actually in the
arena; whose face is marred with sweat and dust
and blood; who strives valiantly; who errs and comes
short again and again; who knows the great
enthusiasms, the great devotions and spends
himself in a worthy cause and who, if he fails, at
least fails while bearing greatly so that his place
shall never be with those cold and timid souls who
know neither victory nor defeat.
—Theodore Roosevelt

being happy and pursuing your dreams is
not the run-of-the-mill path to follow in life. Mostly, people
start off with lots of dreams, then make lots of compro-
mises, get caught up in situations they didn't intend, then
just go along for the ride, making the most of it. That's why

the illegal drug industry is so strong. Escape from time to time is a necessary requirement of an unfulfilled life.

Don't believe that pursuing dreams is a bed of roses, though. Get serious, accept that the challenge of pursuing freedom will be met with aversion from many people along the road.

Jealousy in others may drive them to do and say negative things. Anger at the self for failing to pursue life passions can be a very destructive thing.

Pursuing the things that are most important to you in life, and not alienating everyone along the way, requires compassion and the ability to grow. Selfish pursuit of goals will only limit us to an egocentric view of the world, and this is where balance comes in.

Balance, so you can determine who you are "being" while you are "doing." There's no point being successful and world famous if you are an asshole because it's almost guaranteed that you'll be unhappy, and there's the catch. Being unhappy would defeat the whole purpose of the exercise.

Get serious but be kind, pursue your goals but embrace unity and oneness.

BE

one

we're all in this together

A human being is part of the whole called by us "Universe," a part limited in time and space. He experiences himself, his thoughts and feelings as something separated from the rest, a kind of optical delusion of his consciousness. This delusion is a kind of prison for us, restricting us to our personal desires and to affection for a few persons nearest us. Our task must be to free ourselves from this prison by widening our circle of compassion to embrace all living creatures and the whole of nature in its beauty.

—Albert Einstein

einstein had a few good ideas and he was on the money here too. A life limited to the self is a limited life indeed. The trick is the spirit in which you do it.

The Buddhists teach that before we can help others we must first help ourselves. Why? Because we may lead people up the proverbial garden path, or we may be pulled down ourselves. Even the airlines tell us that. You know, as the plane is taxiing down to the end of the runway during the safety briefing (the one that no one listens to) they say, "In the event of a loss of cabin pressure, oxygen masks will fall from the overhead compartments . . . Be sure to place one over your own head before you attempt to help others."

Accept that you will die just as quickly as anyone else, don't be fooled into thinking you're any better than anyone else.

In life maybe that should be, "In the event of a total loss of direction in life, be sure to sort out your own shit before you start telling other people what to do."

It's a common delusion and one person in particular comes to my mind as a prime example. Margaret worked with homeless people and spent many hours at a homeless shelter sorting out people's lives and telling people what to do in a very functional sense. What I mean is that she knew where to go to get food and who to approach to organize jobs.

At the end of the day she would go home, collapse into a chair, and have a few stiff scotches. Outside of the shelter, her life was empty. She could help people functionally but she couldn't help them, or herself, emotionally or spiritually. She was as lost and unhappy as they were. Remember how like attracts like? In her own mind she justified her unhappiness by the work that she was doing. Her self-esteem was linked to the things that she was "doing," not by how she was "being." So as soon as she stopped "doing" she was left with the sinking, empty feeling and then she went downhill fast. To deal with it she'd have a few drinks to escape.

The problem was that she saw herself as being better than them on some level, so she held herself separate. But right in front of her was the means to her salvation. If she had bothered to look around and open herself up, she would have realized that a whole lot of people there thought the world of her and would do anything to help her. She was suffocating as she told people to put their masks on, having neglected to put her own on first.

I'm not saying she should stop working with homeless people, far from it. What I am saying is that we're all in this together. At the end of the day nobody is better or worse than anyone else. We are all the same, a common thread runs through us.

In Africa, the Zulus believe, "I am because we are." When they say "Hello" they say "Sawubona" which means "I see you." In other words, "I see you and I recognize

your unique existence." The worst insult you can pay to a Zulu is to not acknowledge their presence. Effectively you are saying to them "In my eyes you do not exist."

I lived in the Drakensberg Mountains in South Africa for a while, and had a good chance to try this out. I was lucky enough to stay on a beautiful farm at the base of the mountains where the overwhelming majority of people were Zulu. Once a week or so I used to drive the thirty kilometers into town. As I passed people walking along the road—which in Africa is a lot of people—I used to wave to them. Now if you did that in Western countries, maybe ten percent of people would wave back. But in Africa, over ninety percent of people wave back. One day a friend was traveling with me and he saw me waving to all these people.

"Do you know those people?" he asked. Before I'd even thought about it, I replied, "I know everyone on some level." I don't know where that realization came from but it hit me like a brick. On some level we do know everyone else, on some level we are all interconnected.

If we can acknowledge this and go beyond the limited notion of the self then amazing things begin to happen. For starters, any sense of loneliness falls by the wayside. How can you be lonely if you are surrounded by people you know? If we can find the courage to let go of this sense of separation we open ourselves up to much greater possibilities. Life expands.

But how much attachment do we have in our world to the notion of "I?" In Africa there has always been a tribal thing going on. To survive in such a place, with other hostile tribes and dangerous animals, it made no sense to be separate. But here, in the "developed" world, we've had a lot of practice in nurturing the notion of "I." If we go back again to Socrates, Plato, and Aristotle, they were all about separation. Not only were they separating things into categories and classifying the world, they were also separating and classifying people. Just have a look at Plato's *Republic* if you want an example.

Philosophers over the years have also built on the notion of existence from an individual perspective. Descartes wrote "Cognitio ergo sum:" "I think therefore I am." It wasn't "We think therefore we are," it was "I." Freud also did a lot of thinking and writing about the notion of "I" and this is the basis for much of our knowledge about the human psyche. Over the ages, the ego has dominated Western philosophical thinking. But how much of it is about dividing up the cake? Starting from a position of scarcity, and then cutting, slicing, and analyzing? Most of it, I would say. Little of it acknowledges the common link between us all, except from a cognitive perspective.

From the perspective of the linear and analytical thinking espoused by these people, we're in a weird situation. There's a lot of wealth in the world. For the most part in

Western society, we've removed the threat of starvation and other life and death issues. Everything should be rosy. But it's not. As I've already noted, there is a rise in the incidence of depression in the Western world that threatens to become an epidemic. Freudian psychology says, "Analyze them and find out what went wrong in their upbringing, then find a solution and fix them." Other scientists look at the chemicals in the brain and say, "Aha, it seems that they are depressed because they are not producing enough x. Give them this pill and they will be fine in an hour or so."

That sort of thinking is like fixing a machine. Find out what's wrong, make the repairs and put it back into service. If it's human, analyze it, decide what's wrong, put it back into the economic machine, keep it going, keep it desiring, keep it working to fulfill its desires. When it does it will be happy.

NO. Doesn't work.

I know people who have been taking antidepressant medication for years. There's nothing wrong with taking medication to correct an imbalance. The problem occurs if that's all you do. You need to take action to move things forward and change who you are being.

Limit your life to concentration on the self and your world can only be small. Embrace interconnectedness and unity and the world becomes endlessly full of possibilities.

BE

But what fights against this notion? What part of us recoils at the thought? Our ego screams, "What about me?"

Our egos want to be better than others, to have more than them, to be acknowledged by them. Our egos are the source of our desires but also the source of our unhappiness. When others are down, secretly, deep inside of us, some part relishes the fact. Because in a win/lose world it can only mean that we are up. When we are down, some part of us reviles against telling others because it is admitting our weakness.

This type of thinking has often been viewed by philosophers and psychologists over the years as "human nature." Any altruistic acts are seen as aberrations. True human nature is driven by greed, they say. Because of "human nature" people in societies have to be controlled. We can't trust people to look after each other, therefore we must put rules in place and enforce them. It is for the common good—so that people will not harm each other. Give up individual freedom for a better society.

The problem is that we have created a world in which freedom relates very strongly to our ability to escape from the clutches of the economic system. If you are incredibly wealthy you can do almost anything. Nobody tells you what to do. In fact, if you want things changed, waving a roll of banknotes will move things along quite nicely.

Let's face it. It suits a small group of people to keep things exactly the way they are now. It suits a small group of people to have everyone else fighting against each other. It suits a small group of people to have everyone believe that human nature is so bad that essentially we cannot be trusted to look after each other. It suits a small group of people to promote the notion of scarcity.

What do they get?

Power. Power through control. Control through the mechanisms of our economic and social systems. Control through fear of what might happen if things were different and everyone was free to do as they please. If enough people fear that then they will be willing to forego some of their freedom for a safe society.

Watch the news at night and count how many stories illustrate the "bad" side of human nature and how many illustrate the "good" side. It all helps to promote the view that the world is a scary place and that we need restrictive systems and rules to make sure everyone doesn't hurt each other.

How to change things?

Reclaim your freedom. Pursue your dreams. Embrace Unity and Interconnectedness.

A world built on abundance can only be abundant. A world built on scarcity can only be scarce. If enough people believe in the abundant nature of the world it will be created. If we want to change the world we must first change ourselves. We are all in this together.

time to evolve

> There is nothing more difficult to carry out, nor
> more doubtful of success, nor more dangerous to
> handle, than to initiate a new order of things. For
> the reformer has enemies in all those who profit
> by the old order, and only lukewarm defenders in
> all those who would profit by the new.
> —Machiavelli

fear has always stopped us from evolving to a whole new level. Fear that if I stop guarding my turf then someone else will take it. Fear that if I stop protecting myself then someone else will hurt me. Fear that if I give, I may not receive something back.

Fear means that we clutch onto life so tightly that we cannot pursue new things and allow them into our lives.

Consider it from this perspective. We are always full, so to allow something new into our lives we must first be willing to create some space by letting something go. Remember the analogy of the computer with the fixed amount of memory—this is the same thing. If we are full of fear then we cannot even consider other possibilities.

It's the same fear that drives people in the business world to work sixty- and seventy-hour weeks. It's the same fear that drives political leaders to negotiate trade agreements with other countries that confer some right to privileged conditions.

Our economic system should serve us, but it directs us. Instead of creating the kind of society we want and then using the economic system to help us deliver it, we find ourselves with our hands tied. How often do you hear political leaders say, "We'd like to be able to spend more money on education but economic conditions do not allow it?"

Ha! What a crock! It will never allow it! By its nature the economic system is built on rational thinking. It divides things up and analyzes them. It can only be linear. It will only deliver things that are already in the pipeline.

Look at it this way. The total value of the companies listed on the stock market is whatever we collectively believe it to be. If we collectively decide that things are looking up and companies should be valued more highly, then they are. If we collectively decide that things are going to get worse, then we can decrease the value of the market.

Do you get it? Nothing stops us from doing either thing, except belief. If we believe in abundance then we can create abundance. If we believe that there are limited resources and that some people should starve, then they do.

I used to trade stocks and futures in Japan and in 1990 the Japanese market was at an all-time high. Stocks were trading at a price-to-earnings ratio of up to a hundred, when traditionally they'd only traded at twenty to forty. But investors believed that the future looked rosy so the market kept going up. Then slowly but surely, some people started to say that the market was too high and eventually this view spread. People started to sell stocks and as the prices went down there was more and more evidence to support the view that the market was over-valued. In the end, that view prevailed and the market fell by more than a half.

The point is that it's all just a result of collective belief. Change the belief, change the result.

We need to get out of this vicious cycle. We need to start interacting with the system in a different way. A way that reflects the type of world that we wish to create rather than the type of world that we have.

Time to evolve

In approximately twenty years the world will be full. Some estimates are that we will have reached a population of about nine billion people and it will be stable for a while and then begin to fall.

Just consider that for a moment. A flat population that will be older on average than it is now and have less children. Will we still accept a situation where a small percentage of the population keeps getting richer and richer while a much larger percentage wallows in poverty?

We need to start embracing a world built on the principles of abundance, unity, and a richness of spirit that is missing in many Western nations. This takes courage and vision, but most of all it takes ACTION.

survival of
the fittest?

We are all leaders. Each one of us is
setting an example for someone else, and
each one of us has responsibility to shape
the future as we wish it to be.
—Keshavan Nair

do you live your life with a "survival of the fittest" mentality? Would you trample over the bodies of others to claim the prize? Do you assume that every conflict you face can only be resolved by someone winning and someone losing?

No?

Then why automatically assume that these are the rules of the game?

Think about it for a second. As we grow up we are told that we should look after our family and friends and we actively nurture their well-being. In many cases we act altruistically for their benefit. Our family and friends give us a safe haven from the outside world. Even when we are arguing we know that the bonds of blood cannot be broken. In other words, we are stuck with each other, so we act in tune with the long-term nature of the relationship.

Now contrast this with the things we are told about the outside world and the business world in particular. "It's a dog-eat-dog world," we say. "Take care" is a common parting phrase. When business people meet for a drink the conversation goes along the lines of a battle report. How are things going? Are you winning or losing? Specific tales that are recounted include great battles that have been won, foes that have been outwitted, challenges that have been met.

We assume that this is just the way of the world. We assume that it can't be changed, so we adapt ourselves to fit in. We are one type of person at home and with our friends, but another when we move into the corporate world.

Why do we assume that it can't be changed?

Stop for a second and think about it from a personal perspective. Are you one person at home and another at

work? Is your guard up when you enter the office? Are you always looking for opportunities that will benefit your organization to the detriment of another?

If like attracts like and collective belief creates reality, then as long as everyone just keeps following along it will always be the same. We will all keep whining and complaining but nothing will change.

If like attracts like, then why not lead instead of follow? Start looking for win/win solutions, embrace an abundant outlook that seeks common good for the benefit of all, not personal good for the benefit of you alone. Evolve to a higher level and lead, don't follow.

time for new ideas

I know all this might seem a bit much, all a bit too radical you might say. But consider this. Our society is still based on the views of people who lived over two thousand years ago. Yes, it's those three Greek philosophers again—Plato, Socrates, and Aristotle.

Our economic system of exchange is based on the ideas of people who lived well over two hundred years ago, the first among them being Adam Smith, the father of free market theory.

Now, all of these ideas have obviously served us well because, fundamentally, things have progressed upward on a linear path. Over the last hundred years in particular it has been fair to assume that each generation would have better prospects than their predecessors. Until now. . . .

Now we are faced with increased levels of depression and suicide, increased levels of stress, and decreased levels of happiness. In addition, as I mentioned previously, we are close to the time when the Earth will reach its maximum population.

Time for some new ideas. The most fundamental of which is a reassessment of basic human nature. Ask yourself, are you driven by your base, animal urges? Or by your higher self? Are you being swung around by the monkey? Or do you think you can direct the monkey? Do you believe that you are bound and limited by your survival needs? Or can you rise above them? Are you fundamentally bad? Or good?

If you believe that you can change and evolve, then why can't we all?

This is the challenge facing the human race now.

To ensure your own freedom you must fight for the freedom of others. Their freedom *is* your freedom.

Okay, so I'm going to stop harping on about this stuff now and look at the implications of changing the way you are being, and getting beyond the self.

the keys to compassion

embracing the notion of inter-connectedness and unity has a profound effect on the way you can be in this world. While we believe that we are separate, we fight our battles by ourselves and struggle alone. Face it, you can only lose yourself if you first believe in the delusion of separation. If you let go of the idea of being separate, then you can never lose yourself. Everything that happens right now is a part of you, and you of it.

The idea of separation results in, and arises from, judgment. Judgment about who is better or worse, judgment about what is right and wrong, judgment about what is good or bad. Let go of judgment and you can begin to embrace all experience as part of the whole. Hold on to judgment and you put others into boxes and push them

away. Because like attracts like, if you judge others and push them away, they will do the same to you. You might end up feeling very smug and right about things but you will be on a very lonely island. One that will give you no mirrors to see yourself and to develop.

You know the type of people I mean. Strong, opinionated people who have a view about everything and are so fixed and rigid in their ideas that they will never change. I believe that as we grow older we all reach a point in life where we decide either to rest on what we know and effectively stop our development, or to continue growing and learning, opening our minds up to endless possibilities. If you decide to stop and close your mind then you give yourself nowhere to move to. If this is what you want to do then go right ahead but it will provide you with increasing levels of bitterness and frustration as time passes.

Go back to the past/present/future model and you will see that it means you have staked out a bit of turf in the past domain and decided to just keep perpetuating this into the present. People who do this end up having so much invested in this position that they find it increasingly difficult to move. If they come across people who disagree with them about anything, they get extremely angry because they don't know what else to do.

This view of the world is one that arises from the type of thinking that categorizes things. It says that the world should be one particular way and if it is not there is some-

thing wrong. The first thing these people look for is something or someone to blame.

Turn it around and accept that the world just is. But, most importantly, realize also that the world is constantly moving and changing. See the possibilities, not the problems.

Compassion is about being able to accept all views of the world without judging. If you are clear and secure in who you are and what you are about then you have no reason to put others down or seek to prove them wrong. If you accept that the world is a mystery then you can be big enough to embrace other people's views of the world and uplift them.

If you have a fixed view of the world then all you can do is constantly seek to put forward or defend this view. Your outlook is premised on the idea that the world is fixed. Even scientists now know that this is untrue. From a scientific perspective, the universe is constantly expanding. If this is the case then why can't human consciousness be continually expanding?

If you see the world as a constant ebb and flow of energy that is abundant and mysterious, then life is more like a journey across an ocean than a ride on a train. On the train, the tracks are fixed, you have no control and can only sit back and be carried along. If you are journeying across the ocean, you are subject to the whims of the waves, the current, and the weather. So, you need to

know where you are going, what your reference points are and how you are going to deal with emergencies. It might be a wild ride but I can guarantee you one thing—it will be much more interesting than sitting back on the train and staring out the window in a haze of boredom.

So, back to compassion. Take the time to work out who you are and what you are doing but then get beyond it and embrace the interconnectedness of all things. If you can do this, then there will be a big space in your heart for you to embrace other people's views of the world. When you can do this, you can truly connect with other people and truly listen to them.

The best gift that we can give other people is our whole selves in truth. By doing so we give them a true and accurate mirror that allows them to see themselves. We also give ourselves the best opportunity to grow.

pride blinds us

was talking with a friend recently about this whole idea of interconnectedness and oneness and she was quite upset by the idea. Initially I couldn't understand why, then we spoke some more and I realized it was because she felt that if we are all one then nothing was just her. She wanted something to be just her.

The idea of unity doesn't preclude the uniqueness in all of us. Indeed, it relies on it. It means that there is a common element that runs through everything. We are like little balls of energy with a common current running through us all. If one or all of us try to hold onto a bit of the current for ourselves, then instead of being one big glowing light we become a multitude of little globes. Imagine that we are like Christmas tree lights. If you put up a whole lot of individual lights they look good but they

aren't coordinated in any way. You wouldn't win the prize for best lights in the street with a setup like that! To have great Christmas decorations you've got to hang lots of globes together so they project a united radiance. Then each globe is part of something much bigger than itself. The result is much bigger than the sum of the parts.

Being human is a lot like that. We can try to shine individually and we may look good but we will never be as great as we can be when we join with others.

Our pride sometimes blinds us to this possibility. If we think we are better or worse than anyone else then we set ourselves up for a fall. Having an overwhelming sense of self-importance can blind us to the lessons that are right in front of us and prevent us from learning, growing, and moving forward. A sense of self-importance can also be the source of huge unhappiness when it becomes self-pity. Sound strange? Then think about it like this. If you have self pity then you believe that others should feel sorry for you and you think that you are too good for the things that the world has placed right in front of you. In other words, feel sorry for me because I have to work my way through university while all these other people get supported by their parents. The underlying message is, "I'm too good for this, I deserve better."

The world "is"—remember? Something is not good or bad, until we make it so. Self pity is a way of refusing to play the game of life and saying the rules should be bent to accommodate you. It doesn't work that way. Whatever is right in front of you now *is* right in front of you now and the only way to move forward is to take action. Remember that we cannot possibly know the significance of events that are happening now until they become the past. The only thing we can do is put one hundred percent into the here and now and get on with it.

Our pride and sense of self-importance can blind us to this reality and to the opportunities that lie right in front of us.

Consider this example. Bill is a fantastic scuba diving instructor so he traveled to far north Queensland, Australia to get a job on a boat. When he arrived there it was the height of the season and all the jobs were taken. Despite asking all the boat operators he was unable to get any work. Down to his last few pennies he eventually had to swallow his pride and go to the Social Security office. With all the people in town they immediately found him a job as a limo driver.

Bill didn't want to be a limo driver. As far as he was concerned, limo drivers were no better than glorified taxi drivers. Despite the big chip on his shoulder, Bill was friendly to everyone who got into his limo. As they asked him question after question about the local area, he learned more and more. One day he picked up an English gentleman from the airport and during the hour-long drive to the resort, the passenger asked him all about what

was going on in the area. Bill gladly and cheerfully answered all of his queries and as they neared the resort the passenger was very grateful.

As they drove up the driveway, Bill asked him what he was doing here, to which he replied, "I've just come down from London to launch a new charter boat. It's a pity you're not a diver as we could use someone with your knowledge to run the diving side of things."

I'm sure I don't have to explain to you that Bill's eyes lit up and he got the job and lived happily ever after.

The point?

Well, don't imagine that you know better than spirit. The world is a mystery, remember. What is placed in front of you will be right for you right now, but if you are full of pride you may miss it completely.

life expands

you might have worked out by now that the question of finding direction in life may be answered many times over. This is because life is not the linear, fixed thing that we have been led to believe. Life expands as we live it and as such it is the primary tool on our journey.

The choices we make are elements of this tool. Every choice we make has an effect on the journey and an effect on our life. That's why fate can't be right. We change the world by how we interact with it. Look back on your life and you will see that this is so.

Once you try something you can never turn back, you can never take the experience away. Just by doing something you influence your life in a profound way.

Man's mind, once stretched by a new
idea, never regains its original dimensions.
—Oliver Wendell Holmes

Let's go back to that analogy about rain falling on the plain forming channels and you'll see what I mean. Imagine now that a construction company comes along and decides to dig a big drainage ditch in the middle of the plain. When it rains the water will flow straight into it and things will never be the same again.

Our minds are the same. I learned long division at school, then somewhere along the line I got a calculator. Now I'd struggle to do long division, even if you paid me. Furthermore I couldn't see the point in the struggle and I'd search for a calculator instead.

We are what we repeatedly do.
Excellence then, is not an act but a habit.
—Aristotle

What about this example. What did you do to blow off steam before you started drinking? As teenagers my brothers and I used to ride motorbikes. Next to our house we had a dirt access road and when I used to get wound up I'd jump on the motorbike and zoom up and down the dirt road, pulling wheelies and generally being a badass. When I moved out of home and into a shared house I replaced riding my motorbike with going down to the bar with my friends.

Why is it so difficult now to go down to the bar for a meal with friends without having a drink? If you'd never had a drink in the first place then you'd never know but because you did have that first drink you can't ever go back, your life has changed forever. Same deal with any other drug but probably the most insidious is smoking.

I started smoking when I was fourteen years old because I thought it was cool and all my rebellious friends were doing it. By the time I realized how bad it was for me I'd been smoking for a number of years and the behavioral ruts in my brain were very deep. Now I haven't had a cigarette for a while but I still think about it and know exactly how it feels. I know people who gave up smoking ten years ago and they still crave a cigarette. Again, if they'd never had the first one they wouldn't know what they're missing. Their life has changed forever.

See what I mean? We don't understand the significance of the things we do right now until time has gone by and they have become the past. In this way, life itself is the tool in the journey.

Look at your relationships and you'll see what I mean. By having relationships with people we learn things and they change the ideas that we have in our minds. Our expectations change, our experiences change, our perceptions change. Just by living, we change.

What to take out of this?

Well, I suppose what I'm trying to say is this—don't hold on too tight. If you see the world as an ever-changing ebb and flow of energy, then holding onto a certain fixed idea or view is like trying to hold onto a reed in the middle of a raging river. You can't hold on for long so you may as well let go. And there's the paradox . . . As you're being thrown about by the current you need to not only be willing to let things go but also have some idea where you're going. If you can do this then as the opportunities come racing toward you, you can reach out and grab them with both hands.

> The bird of paradise alights
> from the hand that does not grasp.
> —Wordsworth

the journey is
the destination

in our rush and hustle and bustle we are always looking forward to something or looking back. Rarely are we
right here, right now, but that's the real challenge. As I've
already noted, we tend to look at life as a linear progres-
sion, straight line, unidirectional, and this tends to screw
us up.

No matter what we come across in the here and now,
we tend to look at it only as a stepping stone to something else.

This story of a young Japanese boy wanting to learn
martial arts illustrates this. Tetsuro was small for his age
and was often picked on by the other boys in his village.
One day he decided to learn martial arts to protect himself so he asked around and found that there was a great
Sensei living nearby in the mountains. Tetsuro set off to

see the Sensei to become a great warrior. After several days' travel he arrived at the Dojo, greeted the Sensei, and told him that he wished to join the Dojo. The Sensei was pleased and Tetsuro was very eager to learn.

"How long will it take me to be a black belt, Sensei?" he asked.

"Ten years," replied the Sensei.

Tetsuro was disappointed, he didn't want to wait that long.

"What if I work twice as hard as the other boys, how long will it take then?"

"Twenty years," the Sensei replied.

Tetsuro was confused.

"What if I work twice as hard as the other boys and stay up late and work during the night, how long will it take then?"

"Thirty years,'"replied the Sensei.

Tetsuro didn't understand.

"Sensei, why do you say it will take longer if I work harder?" The Sensei looked down at him thoughtfully, then said, "Because if you have one eye on the destination you only have one eye on the journey."

We need to keep our destination in our mind's eye so that we can be fully present to the moment and make full use of the power that we have in the present. Only by doing this can we be fully aware of our current actions and have the presence of mind to see the opportunities that arise along the way.

Tricky, eh? Have a clear idea of where you want to go but then be fully present to the here and now.

Have a look at nature though. Is there an end point in nature? No. Everything in nature is in constant flux and change. Remember the Heisenberg principle? The nature of an object is changed by its interaction with the subject. Well here's another theory for you—the Mandelbrot set. The theory is that everything is constantly going from a state of chaos to a state of order, then back into chaos and so forth. The Mandelbrot set is a set of numbers that predicts this.

Think about the implications of that for a second. Everything is in a state of change the whole time, nothing stays still. For a while a state of order exists. But as it changes it heads closer to chaos, then as the chaos changes it slowly finds a new but different state of order.

Now combine together the Heisenberg principle and the Mandelbrot set.

Everything is always changing. As we interact with our environment we influence it and cause it to change. The way it changes is directly related to the way that we interact with it. So, the way we see ourselves changes the way that we change. The intentions that we put out into the world influence the way the world changes. We become what we believe.

Remember Descartes said, "I think therefore I am." Maybe instead it should be, "I believe therefore I am."

The ancient tribes in the South American jungles, such as the Shuar, Otavalans, and Salasacans, believe in much the same thing. They say that our dreams create our reality, so we can only create a reality that we can first dream. To change our reality all we have to do is change the dream.

So, come back to the journey. It is the destination. The challenge is to have clear intent, but then be totally present to what is happening right now.

bringing it
all together

maybe your head is ready to explode
now? Maybe not? But it's time to put it all together.

This is what I believe.

- The world is a mystery. We should never stop seeking answers but we should never expect to fully comprehend it.

- Yes, there is a purpose to life. It's all about growing, learning, and evolving from the challenges that are placed in front of us. The best way that we can align ourselves to this is to find our life path, or purpose.

BE

- Passion points to purpose. Find the space to disconnect from the world and stop the noise so that you can hear what is really going on deep within you. Search deep and find your passions.

- Embrace death as your adviser. Don't be suckered into thinking you're immortal because, let's face it, you're not. Embracing death will provide a direction and power that come from letting go of the trivialities of life.

- Work out what you believe in and have the courage to stand up for it. Every challenge will make you stronger by delivering a gift of power.

- Set your intention to be happy.

- Do it. The world is all about movement. Action causes ripples that have effects that you can't even start to imagine. Use your new anchor points to create what you really want, not what you're stuck with.

- Break out of the box and embrace abundance.

- Get really good at picking yourself up and dusting yourself off when you get knocked down. Accept it as a part of life.

- Don't be limited by the self. Embrace unity, interconnectedness, and oneness.

- Fight for the freedom of others because their freedom is your freedom. Be brave enough to lead in creating a better, fairer, and freer world.

- Let your life expand. Don't hold on too tight.

- Be fully present in the here and now.

- Hold joy in your heart and put as much positive energy into the world as you can.

Well, there you go, we've got to the end of this little book. For you and for me it's time to step up to the plate and take a swing. I hope these ideas have been useful to you and I wish you well on your own journey.

> At the end of all our journeying we
> shall return to the place from which we
> started and know it for the first time.
> —Four Quartets, T. S. Eliot